A JUNKIE'S NIGHTMARE:

COMING CLEAN

Freddie Jay

This is a true story, but the names have been changed to protect the not-so-innocent. All opinions in this book are those of the author and are not intended as treatment for addiction or anything else.

©2013 Clean Dreams Publishing. All Rights Reserved.

Foreword

My earliest memories of Freddie Jay aren't very good. Before he and I became friends, all I knew of him were the things I heard around the neighborhood. People said the whole family was crazy. When I did meet Freddie, I didn't like him. I was into sports, and it was common knowledge he was into drugs. His father was a well-known dope dealer supplying our neighborhood pillheads, and Fred's brothers were said to be killers. It seemed his mother was the only one who was normal in the family. It seemed to me Freddie Jay didn't have a chance, like he was destined for failure. I'd see him walking around the neighborhood high as a kite, ready to fight anyone who stepped in his way.

Fred and I had nothing in common until I started getting high. The first time I went over his house, we smoked hash right in front of his parents! As we became friends, I could see the danger Fred was in. There were guns, drugs and lots of money in that little house. I came to see a different person than what I'd heard about. Fred was a great friend, and I cherished our friendship. We stuck together; I had his back, he had mine and you very rarely saw us apart. We trusted each other with our lives, even though my family and friends would tell me to stay away from him 'cause he was a young drug addict with an attitude problem.

They didn't see the other side of Fred. We became blood brothers, actually slicing our palms with a razor and shaking hands. I knew Fred had a lot of problems, but our friendship wasn't one of them. He wanted everyone to think he was a super badass. Both his brothers were killers doing long stretches, and I got the idea Freddie Jay wanted to follow in their footsteps. He liked money and drugs and his ego was out of control. He hated school and refused to go most of the time. Om the rare occasion he showed up, we'd cop out by third period to get high. It seemed he really only cared about a few things—his mother, our friendship and his reputation. I knew he cared about me and that he loved his mother more than anyone in the world, but I never saw her love him back.

It seemed there were two very different sides to Fred. Around people, he'd flaunt his money and drugs and start fights just to start them. Then there was generous and thoughtful Fred, who'd give you the shirt off his back. I admit he confused me a lot, and the strangest part of this is we were still just kids, 13 or 14, and life was already out of control. Fred always had to do twice as much as everyone else. He was getting high-grade narcotics from his house, and if I took two pills, Freddie Jay took six! I'm ashamed to say that I even helped him shoot up, and he came close to dying many times. He'd shoot up and be high as a kite, but it wasn't good enough, so he'd do more. I'd be scared, but I'd stay with him to make sure he didn't die. I don't know, but I think maybe Freddie Jay wanted to die.

Eventually we drifted apart, He went to prison, which seemed inevitable, and when I ran into him years later, he was selling coke. He asked me to come on board and I did. We sold lots of coke together and made tons of money, but we smoked coke and Fred shot heroin. It got out of control fast. He ended up losing the house, and that was that. I figured I'd get word he was dead or doing life in prison. I loved Fred like a brother, but to be honest, I never figured he'd change. I didn't hear from him for years, but then my brother told me he saw Fred on Facebook and we started communicating again. I was happy to see him doing so well, but I was skeptical at first. Yet it's true—today Freddie Jay is drug free, married to one woman and a loving father. Seeing this made me believe in the power of God.

I was still struggling with drugs and got in legal trouble again. I was sitting in jail when Fred wrote and asked if he could help in any way. I know from past experience that people disappear on you when you come to prison, but Fred did the opposite. He proved what I already knew—that he was and is a true friend. He has provided me with many letters, words of encouragement and spiritual guidance, not to mention many money orders so I don't starve in here. He has sent me packages to make my stay here a little bit more comfortable. He has had a huge positive effect on me. I always believed in God, but never let Jesus into my heart. I'm now a practicing Christian, and Freddie Jay has been a great inspiration to me—and I'm not the only one he helps. He lives his life to help others and encourages me to do the same. He asks me to help someone in here who is struggling or getting picked on, and I do. Fred is the most giving, caring person I know. He forgives those who hurt him and encourages everyone he meets. Freddie Jay isn't just my friend, he's my brother. I always knew there was more to him, more in his heart, and thanks to God, it's now pouring out of him. He has become a great human being and takes no credit, but gives it all to God. He is the most selfless, giving person I know. The guy everyone thought would OD in the gutter or get life in prison is a great husband, a great father and a successful businessman. I'm proud to know him. He's my spiritual advisor, my best

friend and my brother. His turnaround was made possible the day he let Jesus Christ into his heart. He's a great man loved by many, but he gives all thanks to God.
Chris Royer (a.k.a., Chris Kline)

Chapter 1
Devil's Child

Where do I begin? I guess in the beginning would be best!!

I was born on March 24 in 1968. I don't know what the weather was like; after all, I was just a baby :) so give me a break. And yes, I know I could have googled it, but you're the one who bought a book from a junkie :) I digress!

From the moment I entered this world, I was being pushed and pulled around. The story goes that they left my mother in labor too long, and when they finally got her in the delivery room, they had to use forceps to pull me out. These were olden days, people, where they still used such archaic practices. So I was battered and bruised with a head a bit more misshapen then most when they brought the family to the nursery to view their bundle of joy, through the glass, (yep, they still did that, too). So while my sister "oohed" and "aahed" about my little fingers and little toes, my dad uttered a line way before Arnold Schwarzeneggar made it famous in the movie *Predator*, "That's one ugly muthafucker!" That was my "Welcome to the world, Freddie!"

I was the last born, having two brothers and a sister before me. Legend holds that I was conceived at a little motel called the Shade and Rest while my parents were down South to watch the murder trial of my oldest brother. Here's a little background on that: Seems my oldest brother, John, had gotten in some minor trouble in Maryland, so he and two friends decided to flee prosecution by running to Florida. I don't know what the trouble was or what the plan was, but John certainly wasn't the brightest 18 year old, and I gather his friends were equally challenged. They made it as far as Columbia, South Carolina, before running out of money and resources. Again, the trio put their vast knowledge to work and elected to rob a fruit stand to fund this less then successful attempt to abscond. The man at the fruit stand didn't want to give up his hard-earned money and pulled a shotgun. My brother's friend was shot in the face, and my brother stabbed the man. The man died, but John's friend lived. John was sentenced to life and a day, and I wish that was where his story ended, but we will talk more about him later on.

After a few days at the hospital, they brought me home and put me in the care of my sister, who was 17 at the time of my birth. I imagine it hurt her social life, but my mother couldn't be bothered with such things. She already had the apple of her eye in my older brother, Steve. Did you just hear angels sing? Me neither, but my mom was convinced that Steve was a gift straight from heaven. Of course, opinions vary; more on that later. There I was, just a baby being raised by a 17-year-old girl. Now, in 1968, it wasn't popular to be an unwed mother, and a 17-year-old mother was really looked down on. So I'm sure my sister got some strange looks from the general public who were not aware she had charge of her youngest sibling. What I didn't know was that in a few short years, my world would be turned upside down and my later issues with fear and abandonment would get their roots in decision made by my sister's relationship with the fearless leader of our clan—enter Steve Apostoledes, Sr.!!!

My father. Wow, what a tough character to put on paper! I've put off writing this book for fear that people would think that my father was a work of an overactive imagination, but the truth is, I'm not talented enough to make up such a guy. He was an ultraviolent, mean, cruel, kind and compassionate walking contradiction! I know that no person is the same all the time. We are emotional creatures given to our feelings at any given moment, but this guy was extreme in every sense of the word. He could give a complete stranger the shirt off his back, then come home and beat his wife and kids without a hint of sadness or sorrow afterwards! A complex man to say the least: a hard drinker, a barroom brawler, a woman beater, a child abuser... yes, he was all these things. And he also was a good provider, a guy you could count on, had a wicked sense of humor and an incredibly likable guy! He came to my Little League games on occasion, and in many ways tried to make up for the mistakes he made with my older siblings. But my father had his addictions, so history was sure to repeat itself each and every time he fell off the wagon. I'm sure if this book is to be a best seller, it will be due to him and his antics, or at least in part.

My dad wasn't in the mafia, but he certainly lived like a gangster. There were always a half dozen of his boys around, with colorful names like Teddy "Two Guns" or Bruce "The Jew." Everyone called my father "Greek." It wasn't unusual to wake up in the middle of the night to see guys dragging stolen goods in or splitting up stacks of cash at our kitchen table. One morning, a schoolmate came over to walk to school with me. I had a hard time explaining why my dad's friends were all crashed out on the floor and there was something like ninety cases of beer stacked in our living room and kitchen! It was business as usual at my house; there was always fights fueled by alcohol and drugs. My brother Steve was getting older, and him and Dad were fighting and arguing all the time, some of them very scary and some of them incredibly funny.

One of the funny incidents happened on a summer night in 1977. My father and brother started out drinking together, which led to arguing, which led to punches. My brother hit the old man and ran out the door. My father grabbed one of the cheap knives out of the steak knife drawer and ran after him. By the time my dad got to the porch, Steve had made it to his truck, where he grabbed two beer bottles from the back and threw them at my dad in quick succession. One bottle hit the knife, breaking off the blade; the other hit my dad in the forehead! My father stood there with a knife handle in one hand and blood trickling down his face as my brother made his getaway, the sounds of *Helter Skelter* coming from his AM radio as he sped off. Most kids would be terrified; for us, it was Thursday.

Don't get me wrong. Growing up in the '70s wasn't all bad. In fact, it was a glorious time—if I could bottle it and sell it, well, I'd never have to work again and could wipe out the national debt! Sure, it was bell bottoms, feathered hair and floppy hats, and yes, the Starland Vocal Band and John Travolta, as well as David Soul, were at the top of the pop charts, but there was also Deep Purple and The Faces; Black Sabbath and Alice Cooper came along with theatrics and the term heavy metal. We had movies like *The Godfather* and *Dog Day Afternoon*. We also saw the end of the Vietnam War. People knew one another, and kids walked into school without having to pass through a metal detector. I guess the '70s was like any other decade; there were good things and bad things, but it was the time I was coming of age, and the '70s will always hold a special place in my heart.

## Chapter 2
## Broken Dreams

In Chapter One, I alluded to a life-changing event. Well, it would be the first of many, but what I couldn't have known is that it would follow me for forty years!! In my dream, I was running from some unknown monster. It was chasing me through trees and over rocks, and as I came to a clearing, my feet came out from under me and I was falling—falling into the darkest pit one can imagine. I screamed for my sister, but she never came. I kept calling her name until I was shook gently awake by my father, who picked me up in his arms and said, "She'll be back, Freddie boy!" What I didn't know, but my subconscious had seen coming, was my sister had run off to marry her boyfriend and I was on my own.

The things that led up to my sister leaving were legion! My father was in his usual form one evening—drunk! My sister was out on a very rare date. It was rare not because she was unattractive; quite the opposite. She was a very attractive young lady, but rare because she had a baby to take care of and my father didn't let her date much. Maybe he didn't want some young man to get what he wanted for himself, but that's not my story to tell. Anyway, when she rushed through the door, my father was one step ahead of her. He had already set the clocks ahead to make her appear late. "Cynthia, what time did I tell you to be in?"

As he moved toward her, she choked out "I'm sorry, Daddy, I thought I was five minutes early."

His empty eyes glazed over and spittle shot out with his roar, "YOU THOUGHT!" In an instant, she was on the ground, having taken two punches directly to the face. He stood over the 75 lb. girl looking like he had just won a heavyweight bout. The look of satisfaction spreading across his face made her hate him, and she knew if she didn't leave, she might end up dead.

That was the final straw, but there had been so many things he had done to that skinny little girl. One story that went around was that when she was smaller, maybe nine or ten, she snuck a puppy in the garage. My father noticed her going out a bit too frequently and went to investigate. He discovered her infraction. "Cindy, come here."

Tears sprung to her eyes. "Daddy, I just…"

He cut her off. "It's OK, Cindy. What's the little guy's name?"

Relief swept through her as a huge smile broke out on her little face "I don't know, Daddy. Maybe Snowball." She reached for the puppy as my father stroked the little fluffy puppy's head. Before my sister could grab the puppy, my father grabbed it by the tail and slammed the dog's head into the block wall. My sister screamed as he swung the defenseless dog into the wall two more times before throwing the dead dog to the ground.

"DON'T YOU FUCKIN' CRY! LOOK AT ME, CINDY. DON'T YOU CRY!" My sister stood there, her face twisted in agony, trying not to cry. My father glared at her. "Now get in the house and go to bed." My sister ran to her room and cried herself to sleep. That was my father: a sick, sick man. And that was my sister, a little girl who to this day still loves her Daddy.

That's just the way life was in my father's house. But the crazy part is both me and my sister loved my father, while we feared and hated him. I could write a thousand books and never make the reader understand this paradox simply because I don't understand it myself. All I can say is my father's incredible cruelty was coupled with incredible generosity and acts of love. We were in a store, and while my dad was paying a bill, I was looking at a stereo. It was a top-of-the line Technics sound system with one of the very first CD players, as well as a cassette player, tuner, amp and turntable. It had four speakers taller than me, and had me smiling from ear to ear. My dad walked over and said, "What did you find there, Freddie boy?" Well, I started rattling off the details—it could slice, it could dice, it was all I ever wanted—and my father, who had A1 credit, said to the salesman, who hadn't said a word, "Ship this to my house, today."

"Sure thing, Mr. Steve, but you do know this system is a little over $1,100?"

My father, in true gangster form, said, "I didn't ask you the price. Now get it on the truck!" My father had his demons; some of them very dark, but he tried to make up for it by giving huge gifts and some would say, buying our love. I guess that's true, but I know my father loved me. He was just a victim of himself and his childhood.

As for my other brother, he was a bad kid and got worse as he got older. He was a true tough guy, and I looked up to him. To me, he always won the fight and always got the girl. I was, and am, a big Western fan, and he was my Clint Eastwood and John Wayne all rolled into one. Too bad he didn't see me as someone to protect. No, he was, and is, a sociopath who has absolutely no feeling for his fellow man. As they say, shit runs downhill, and I was at the bottom of that hill. When Dad beat his ass, Steve would do the manly thing and find someone smaller and weaker to take out his frustrations on, and without my sister there to protect me, I was easy prey. I suffered many beatings at my brother's hands, but I would occasionally get even. One particular time, my brother beat my ass when my parents weren't home and made me sit on the steps where I couldn't see the TV. I sat there slowly plotting my revenge. As my brother lay on the couch dozing while watching *Scooby-Doo*, I asked in my most humble voice, "Stevie, can I get something to drink?"

"Get it and get your ass back on the steps."

I ran to the refrigerator and obediently returned to the steps, where I sat drinking my Coke. Coke back then came in thick, glass bottles. I sat there, just biding my time, when my brother rolled over on the couch with his back to me. I shot a glance at the front door to make sure it was unlocked. It was, so I made my move silently across the floor, the bottle raised over my head. My brother shifted and my heart leapt to my throat. In a moment, I was over him and brought the heavy bottle crashing down on his head. I saw the blood fly, but I was already out the door, running down the street!

Sure that my brother was right on my heels, I ran as fast as my little legs would go. I finally stole a glance over my shoulder and seeing no one, I hid in the bushes for what seemed like hours, till I heard my Dad's voice calling me. I was prepared for the beating I was sure was coming. I walked to my father, and to my surprise, a big smile broke out on my Dad's face. "What happened, Freddie boy?"

"Stevie beat me, and I'm tired of it."

"So what did you do?" My dad laughed the words.

"I hit him with a Coke bottle and ran," I said sheepishly.

My dad was laughing so hard, I guess pleased that his son wouldn't be walked on. "You showed him. He'll think twice before touching you again!"

Well, lucky for me, my brother had lied and said that out of nowhere I walked up and clobbered him—a story my mother believed because if Stevie said it, well, it must be true, but my dad knew that just wasn't in my character. I was considered the "soft one" 'cause I would always avoid confrontation. My father knew that I had grit, but I had to be pushed, and on that day, he couldn't have been prouder of me. To him, it was better than bringing an 'A' home from what he called the "pencil pushers" at school.

Chapter 3
Wango Tango

As Stevie got older and started to challenge my father by calling him "The Greek," I knew it wouldn't be long before he was out of my father's house! I was right, and in 1979, Stevie found a new residence at The Maryland Correctional Institution, where they would give him free room and board for forty three years or until the parole board saw fit!
https://www.google.com/search?q=dundalkeagle.com/scrapbook/32425-compiled-by-deborah-cornely&ie=UTF-8&oe=UTF-8&hl=en&client=safari

The trial lasted three days and ended with Steve being convicted of stabbing a man eleven times in the chest. I believe the charges were as follows: attempted murder, assault with a deadly weapon, use of a weapon in the commission of a felony, yadda, yadda, yadda. My father, the person my brother would later claim never did anything for him, spent $10,000 on lawyers. However, no lawyer could help a guy who, when told he'd be sentenced in thirty days, stood up and told the judge he had waited long enough and demanded to be sentenced immediately! The judge obliged and sentenced him to consecutive sentences totaling 43 years, and then the government tacked on four more for an unrelated charge.

There ya have it. I'm nine years old, I have one brother doing life, another doing 43 years and a sister in the wind. Nothing else could go wrong; hadn't I endured enough? Boom! My mom passes out in the grocery store, and they rush her to the hospital and start running tests! Mom has breast cancer and has to undergo an emergency mastectomy. When they opened her up, the cancer had spread. By year's end, my mother was diagnosed with breast cancer, bone cancer and tumors in her head! She was given six months, possibly a year, to live. I clung to my mother and she, having no one else, clung to me. I basically stopped going to school, but they gave me a home tutor. I didn't have time to be a kid. I had to take care of my sick mother. Looking back, my mother should have been in the hospital, but my father wouldn't have it. He bought a hospital bed, put it in the front room and got her a full-time nurse: me!

What I didn't know at the time was my dad found a way to capitalize on my mother's sickness. She was prescribed some of the strongest painkillers known to man, and my dad quickly found a market to sell them. He wasn't completely heartless; he did buy her Percodan for her pain, but sold her Dilaudid pills that at the time went for $20 a piece on the street. He used his guys, influence and growing bank account to corner the market in our little neighborhood. Pretty soon The Greek was the go-to guy for all your pharmaceutical needs. There were pot and coke dealers, but he was the pill man, and he protected his interests fiercely! In short order, he went from Sunny's Surplus pants and T-shirts to Brooks Brothers. He was fond of a store called The Manor Shop, where he bought clothes an uneducated man would think nice. He wore be-bop hats and Ocean Pacific shirts. He had a few females willing to perform sex acts for a few pills, so he was beginning to believe he was Don Juan. I'll never know all the demons that man lived with.

My mother responded to treatment. The six months they gave her passed, then the year. In fact, she lived thirty-one more years after being given months to live! As 1980 passed, we heard my oldest brother was coming up for parole. Yes, they do things differently down South, or at least they did back then. John came up and was turned down initially, only to be paroled in late '82 or early '83, when my father begrudgingly let him move back home. My father got him a job; John lost it. My father bought him a used car, he wrecked it. He dated some of the ugliest women I've ever laid eyes on, but I guess it was better than the boys he preyed on in prison.

By the time John came home, I was smoking pot and drinking. I didn't really know him, but my father was kinda hard on him, always putting him down. I had heard John had it real rough as a kid. My father wouldn't let Johnny anywhere near his pill stash, but I had open access because my dad was always sending me to get this many or that many when he had a sale. I knew all the stash spots and wasn't shocked when John asked me to steal one of the pills for him. I wanted to impress my oldest brother and win his respect, so I gaffled one of the little pills everyone was paying top dollar for. But I was shocked when I saw my brother take the little pill, crush it up, and put it on a spoon. I watched in fascination as he pulled a syringe from his sock, then drew water up and added the crushed pill. He lit his lighter and put it under the spoon. As the concoction came to a boil, John pulled a small piece of cotton from his Winston cigarette case, dropped it on the spoon, and drew up the yellowish liquid into the syringe. I sat mesmerized as he stuck the needle into his arm, pulled back on the white plunger and a small amount of blood appeared in the yellowish liquid. His hand switched position, and he pressed the plunger down as the liquid disappeared inside his arm. It had an immediate effect; his eyes rolled back and a look of pure ecstasy appeared on his face as he slumped back into the chair. I guess most people would have been horrified, but I wasn't—I was intrigued!

I'm getting a little ahead of myself. Let's go back to the summer of 1981. There would be many firsts that summer. It was the first time I went to a rock concert. I had four tickets to go see Ted Nugent. The Motor City Madman was coming to the Baltimore Civic Center. I invited the two brothers from next door to go with me 'cause they had a car and were older, cool dudes. They were also able to buy alcohol, and I learned to love peppermint schnapps! It deadened my fears and made me something I wasn't. I lived in constant fear—afraid my mom would die, afraid of my dad, afraid of being abandoned, afraid of not being good enough, afraid of failure, afraid of success, afraid of police and the list goes on. Booze gave me the courage to talk to girls and to fight the older guys I hung with. I couldn't see the collision course I was on, and no one was there to guide me. My dad took a strange approach. Rather than be a father, he just overlooked me staggering in at the age of thirteen and told me if I wasn't in the house by 11:00 p.m., the doors were locked till 8am, so get in or stay out. My mother was wracked on prescription pills and had long forgotten the little boy who slept on the couch to take care of her and empty her potty chair. The little boy who went in a Jimmy's Cab to G.B.M.C. five days a week for three months at a time when she was going for cobalt and then chemo therapy.

I was headed for trouble. I was headed for years of pain, but there was no stopping the things set in motion. On our way to the concert, I was drinking my schnapps when one of my 'friends' said "Hey, Freddie, do you know how to roll?" With that, he threw me a bag of weed and rolling papers. As we smoked the joint I had poorly rolled, I thought to myself, *Man, I have some really cool friends.* We went into the concert on a cloud; the party continued inside with 15,000 of my closest friends. I had found me a little rock-and-roll chick to help me smoke my weed and drink my schnapps. We were in the nosebleed section, but that hardly mattered when my rock-and-roll chick started performing fellatio as Terrible Ted tore into *Wango Tango*. So this is what life was. I found my happiness—my place in sex, drugs, rock and roll and alcohol!

Chapter 4
Ain't Talkin' 'Bout Love

Yes, the age thirteen was a serious turning point in my life. I was introduced to rock music and I loved it; I was introduced to sex and I loved it; I was introduced to drugs and I loved them! My friends were changing. I found myself hanging with an older crowd, and since I always had money and drugs, I was popular with them. I was able to keep a cash flow from my father. He couldn't keep his money in the bank, so he used to get me to put it in a lockbox up in the attic. I thought nothing of snagging a hundred here and there. After all, he's the one who taught me to cut corners. I didn't believe there were good people; I figured everyone stole a little bit! Anyway, this kept me in the older crowd. They wanted to party on my money, and I wanted their connections and approval. I didn't hang with kids my age, partly because I was into things they hadn't dreamed of yet and partly because their parents didn't want them around the "Greek's Kid."

I did have a best friend going to school, though. His name was Chris Kline. He lived down the street from me, and we would walk to school smoking weed together. If we saw each other in the hallway between classes we'd be gone, out at the little green bridge smoking pot and laughing. We went to rock concerts together and hung at each other's house after school. Life was one long party, and we embraced it. It was the '80s, and life was good. It's not my place to tell Chris's story, but we had a lot in common, for as different as we were. Chris was real easygoing, but don't press your luck with him, 'cause he was a damn good fighter. We never fought each other, but I'm pretty sure he would have mopped the floor with me. Fortunately, we were brothers who fought together against others. I loved him then, and I love him now. I consider him more of a brother than my biological brothers. Our friendship remains to this day, and I could write a whole book just about our exploits. But this isn't that book. Let's see how well this one does and, well, who knows?

During my teen years, my oldest brother had violated parole a few times, but was always released within a short period of time. I was there for one of his new offenses. He and my father were sitting at the kitchen table one rainy evening when I walked through the door. I was around fifteen years old and still didn't question my father when he told me to grab a can of gas and a bumper jack from the garage and wait for him in the car. I did wonder why we were going on a service call in the car rather than the tow truck my dad owned, but you just didn't question my father. Before long, he and John were in the car, and we were driving in silence, which seemed odd, but so was the fact that John and my father were doing something together. Anyway, I realized it was no service call when we turned on the street and my father instructed John to shut off the lights. "Freddie, when I get out, hand me the bumper jack," my dad barked at me. We pulled up next to a late-model pick-up. In a flash, my dad was out. It took three hits to bust the driver's side window. Next, he was pouring gas in the vehicle's interior. He took a book of matches, lit them and threw them in the truck. With a "fwump!" the truck went up in flames. My dad was back in the car, and we were speeding away. At the top of the street, my mother's oldest son looked back and said "Wow!" as my father and I screamed in unison, "GO!"

I knew the guy's truck my father set on fire. His name was Bell. He had pulled in my dad's driveway about six months before to buy car parts from my father. He and my father had a disagreement that ended up with Mr. Bell being knocked to the ground. He made it to his truck and pulled out to the street, where he got out of his truck with a slingshot and steel ball of all things. My father rushed to the street ready to fight. When he was within a few feet, the man let the ball fly, and it was spot on. It hit my father directly between the eyes, breaking his nose and glasses! My father hands shot up to shield any more possible blows, but Bell headed for the truck he wouldn't drive much longer. It all ended in a mess. My father was in the hospital a couple days. Mr. Bell lost a truck, and Johnny went to the can for a year or so. Someone identified John fleeing the scene. The victim's vision failed him by the time court rolled around, and my dad walked, but John got convicted anyway. John was a pawn in my father's chess game, but we hadn't heard the last of John Julius Lacey Apostoledes!

Again, I'm a little ahead of myself. I wanna take you to a moment in my life I have thought about so many times over the years. I have often wondered how different my life would be if I had never injected drugs. I was around fourteen, maybe fifteen (the years begin to blur because of the drug use, but I know it was in that general time of my life that I first shot up). It was with my oldest brother, John. I had stolen pills from my father and watched him inject them. I told my brother that the only way I would get him anymore was if he hit me with one of them. John never liked me or cared enough to tell me no. I was a bit scared, but I knew that it was stronger than the alcohol or weed I had been doing. If those things were pretty good, surely this would be great! And it was!

It's very hard to describe the feeling of opiates when injected directly into your veins. As my brother pulled the syringe out of my arm, I felt a warmness begin in my feet. It traveled up my body and exploded in my head. It was like stepping out of freezing cold water and having someone wrap a nice warm blanket, just out of the dryer, around you. It's puppy dogs and butterflies. I made my way down the steps to the couch. My father was out, and my mom was asleep in her hospital bed on the first floor. I sat on the couch feeling so good, it didn't matter that my mom was sick; everything would be OK. It didn't matter that my dad was a maniac; everything was super cool. For the very first time in my life, I wasn't afraid! The drug had given me such a wonderful euphoria, but for me the beauty was no fear. I didn't understand, then, that fear dominated my life. It controlled my every thought. I was a teenager crippled by fear, but I thought I had just found a perfect substance that would fix all these things!

No one becomes a heroin junkie overnight, and neither did I. In fact, heroin wouldn't come into play for a few years. I was a kid, but I knew the dangers of using the needle too often. I would take all kinds of pills and drink and smoke and even shoot cocaine or Dilaudid on occasion, but it would be a few years before the needle took hold of me. However, once it did, it would be a trip into an abyss only a few make it back from! For this moment in time, I was king of the world, but I was atop a very fragile throne!

Chapter 5
Crazy from the Heat

The next few years were the years of a troubled boy headed to a troubled future. I got pinched for the first time when I was fifteen. It was a marijuana possession set around an almost comedic set of events. My father helped this lady who bought pills from him get a phone put in her house. She lived on our street, and I guess she had bad credit or whatever. When she didn't pay the bill, my father sent me to take the phone out of her house. I knocked on the door and her son answered. I knew the boy and didn't want to be a jerk, so I said, "Hey, man, my father wants the phone he had put in for your mom. Can you grab it for me?" He didn't know the details anymore then me and just grabbed the phone for me and I left.

I went home and gave my father the phone, and he and my mother, who had improved in health a great deal, left the house to go have dinner. I broke out my bowl and a nickel bag weed, took a few hits and, being a goofy kid, blew the smoke in the direction of the family dog, who snorted and got away from me. Laughing, I looked up to see a Baltimore county police officer looking through the bay window a few feet from me. In a moment, he was at the door demanding I open it. I obeyed, only to be put in handcuffs and taken into custody,

The boy's mom came home and asked what happened to the phone. I suppose the boy, afraid to tell his mother he gave it to me because The Greek wanted his phone back, told her I came in the house and took the phone! For what reason, I don't know, but she called the police, who came to my door just in time to see me blowing pot smoke at my dog. Thank God they couldn't print my name in our neighborhood newspaper because I was still a minor. Of course, everyone who heard the story had a great laugh.

My teen years were filled with drinking, drugging and lots of sexual conquests! I considered myself quite the ladies man. I especially liked exotic dancers. In many of them I found exactly what I was looking for: a pretty face, an incredible body, loose morals and a love for all things narcotic! That's not to say that ALL strippers are like that, but the ones I wanted around me were! It never occurred to me that they never really liked me, just my money and drugs. However, if the thought had crossed my mind, I'm sure it would have made little difference. My thinking at the time was everybody uses everybody, and I certainly didn't respect them.

By the time I was sixteen, I was on my own. My father had caught me stealing from him and took a swing at me. He hit me solid on the side of my face, but I was so stoned on Valium and bootleg Quaaludes that it just barely turned my head, to which I looked at my father and asked, "Is that all you got, old man?"

He allowed me to go to bed, and the next day I thought things were over. Everything seemed normal when he said, "Freddie, is there any of them big trash bags under the sink?" I looked under and informed him that there were two left. He said "Good. Take them upstairs, put your clothes in them and get the fuck out of my house!!!!!"

I stayed with friends and generous females for awhile,

but it's funny how fast they disappear when the money and the drugs run low. After a few months, my father let me return home, only to some very different rules. There were deadbolts on his bedroom door and bars had been welded over the window in the Magnaseal door. There was even a safe in my father's room now! There were guns all over the house, I thought this was an overreaction to me stealing from him, but the truth is, my father was coming undone. He had been diagnosed with schizophrenia years before, and it was only getting worse. He would stop drinking and straighten up for awhile, only to return to it again, with it getting worse each time—if that were possible at this point!

If this were a movie instead of a book, this would be the part where the music plays and a montage of drugs, arrests, arguments, fights, overdoses and the passage of time occurs. Throughout this time, I remained very close to my mother. She enabled me and discounted my behavior because we had a bond. A bond that began when she got sick, I would sit in the waiting room and pray the whole time that her treatments were working. I believed if I prayed the whole time, she would get better. The fear of losing her was more than my little heart could bear, but bear it I did, every day till I discovered opiates! The great drug relieved me of all my fears and made me feel wonderful. I know I keep jumping around; I need to hire an editor to fix these things.

Anyway, by seventeen, I was a nuisance to local law enforcement, who viewed me as a troublemaker, which I was. Most of them really disliked me, but there was one cop who seemed to have a real fondness for giving me a hard time. As I said in the beginning, I changed a lot of names in this book, so let's just call this guy Officer Roberts. He was your quintessential Barney Fife cop, and even resembled the fictional character. This cop knew my brothers and my father. He witnessed firsthand the hell we lived through, yet he never tried to help or reach out. He occasionally locked up my dad, who was back home in a few hours. Laws were different in those days, but Roberts was just a despicable little man who enjoyed hitting a cuffed 16-year-old boy, but lacked the courage to take on a grown man without backup!

It wouldn't be fair to point out the bad cop without pointing out two very good cops. One, whose name was Officer Vicki, as I recall, offered me comfort. They had locked me up one evening, all whacked out on Tuinals and whiskey. I tried to fight the arresting officers (who I wish I knew so I could go back and apologize to them), so they locked me up and took me to the Dundalk police station where Officer Vicki took the handcuffs and shackles off me and gave me something to drink and a cigarette. The man sat and talked to me like a father. I'd like to think he saw past my tough guy act and saw the scared little boy. I was locked up many times in that police station, and that man never talked down to me and always treated me fair. When I was especially combative and saw Officer Vicki, I'd settle down and do what he asked. I'll always remember the first night how he sat for hours, when I'm sure he had other duties, and just talked to me, cracking jokes and treating me like an equal!

The other good cop was a city police officer named Kirhigas, or as he was known, "Chris the Cop." He lived across the alley from me and was more of a father to me then my own father. His son was still small, so Chris would come out back and play basketball with me, and whenever he drew duty at the Baltimore Zoo or Memorial Stadium, he would take me. I was on cloud nine walking through the zoo with him. He taught me how to twirl the nightstick the way cops on the beat do. He was Greek and incredibly handsome and women always found a reason to ask him a question, which he answered with calm authority. I really looked up to him, and he tried to be there for me, but my father and his life had such a strong hold on me I hardly had a chance. I remember being at the ballpark with Chris when a woman asked him if he was my father. He smiled at me and looked back to the lady who blushed and rambled off five more questions. He never did answer her first question, and I used to daydream about being his son. His real son grew up to become a Baltimore city police officer, and I believe he's still on the force. I grew up to be something else.

As a teenager, I gave the local police a hard way to go, and they returned the favor in spades. I met this girl from New York and was running up phone bills when my father and I had a huge blow-out. I pushed him to the ground and stole his bottle of Dilaudid and, in an ironic twist, he called the police on me! I would have laughed if I hadn't seen the list of charges they leveled on me. The top one, strong-arm robbery, carried fifteen years alone, and second degree assault carried ten years, so I had to get out of Baltimore for a little while and think this over. The New York girl said I could come stay with her, so I jumped a Greyhound and headed north.

## Chapter 6
## Sunday Bloody Sunday

New York was a new experience. Drugs were cheaper, and there was wall-to-wall beautiful women, so it wasn't long before I was looking for a better deal. The girl I was staying with had assured me she couldn't get pregnant, and I really wasn't attracted to her, but she was a way out of my current situation. I was in contact with my father, and he was talking to the lawyers trying to get my charges dropped, but I had a probation violation hanging over my head, and the judge wouldn't budge on it. So the lawyers tried to get me into rehab before I went in front of him. I hung up the payphone and headed home. I knew there was trouble when I walked through the door. The girl I was living with questioned me about a girl I was sneaking around with. I admitted to it and a coffee mug missed my head by inches. *Forget this*, I thought. *I'm going back to Baltimore. I don't need this headache; I'd rather be in the can!*

I packed my little bit of clothes and headed for the door, the girlfriend on my heels. Once she saw I wasn't playing she said the two words that would stop me in my tracks, "I'm pregnant!" I couldn't believe my ears. I spun around and looked into her eyes. I knew she wasn't lying, but I demanded proof. I wanted to hear it from a doctor, not some stick you urinate on. I calmed her down and called my father. "Dad, I'm ready to come home. I'll do whatever time I gotta do, but I can't take this anymore." My father got on the phone to the lawyers, got his gun and got in the car with his driver and they came to get me. I had yet to tell him about the girl being pregnant, but I neglected to tell the girl I was still leaving. I had no plan whatsoever till I was seated at my father's kitchen table. My father was one of the cruelest men I know, but he had this set of morals that is hard to explain to the outside world. To say he was crass is an understatement, and he had this melodic quality to his voice I can only compare to Steven Tyler. Even when my father spoke, he sang the words!

All these memories come flooding back to me as I sit here writing this book. I can recall my father's gentle words over the situation with the New York girl. "Freddie, I've seen you with some of the most beautiful girls in this neighborhood. Why did you get that ugly muthafucker pregnant?" Yes, my dad had a way with words, but he insisted that I go back and get her, put her up in an apartment and then turn myself in. He gave me the money to get a ratty little apartment in Essex, Maryland, which, depending on who you ask, is either a step up or a step down from my hometown of Dundalk. I jumped in the car with my dad's driver and some guy who didn't speak a word for the ride up and back. We went to New York and picked up the girl. I'll call her Linda, and drove her to her new digs. She never had a decent place to live, so it was fine with her. My dad came over to make sure she had all she needed and told me that I was to go to the lawyer the next morning.

By the end of the week, I had most of the charges dropped, and the judge who I had the Violation of Probation (VOP) with had mercy and gave me 90 days work release. I had a job painting that I never went to. I would come home and be with Linda every day, and at the end of the week, I'd go see this friend of my father's who gave me a pay stub to show the work-release guards. Are you beginning to see how strange my father was? He would kill puppies in front of us and take us on arson jobs, but when I was in a pinch, he came through! I managed to foul up the sweet deal I had with work release by going in stoned out of my mind on Percocet! I took a handful outside the jail, thinking they would hit me once I got to the cell block, but as luck would have it, the guard who signed me in was eating his lunch, and I had to wait in the bullpen for thirty minutes. I held my composure, and I almost got past them, but the one guard didn't like me and made me submit a urine test, so I had to do my last thirty days in lockup. It was a walk in the park, but my thinking at the time was "they done me wrong." I was a confused young man.

By July, 1988, I was doing pretty well for myself. I had come home to Linda, and within a few weeks, had completely refurnished our place. Outside it was a dump; inside it was a palace. I had become a pretty good "second story man." I would bypass alarms by cutting through the roof of businesses and dropping in. I would then load up all the merchandise and put it in a duffel bag by the door. Once I had all I could take, I'd simply go out the front door. By the time the police responded to the alarm, I was gone. I admit it wasn't very sophisticated, but at the time, I thought I was a mastermind. I would fence the stuff to my father, who would pay next to nothing, but it was all profit, so I didn't care. I was hitting gun shops, but this put the cops on high alert, so I backed off for a month and used my ready money to flip a few packs of coke. Money was coming in and drugs were everywhere. I never noticed how unhappy Linda was because I was too busy with other girls, drugs and the life that chose me.

I never considered getting a job and doing the right thing; it just wasn't for me. In my opinion, only a loser would break his back for two or three hundred a week. After all, I made that in a few minutes. Before you go thinking I was a jerk—and you wouldn't be wrong—consider this: I never had a role model or big brother to show me the right way. From a kid up, I was only taught the right way to do the wrong thing. By ten, I could spot a phony $20 and go through stolen goods to find the marked tools or specialty items that an owner could identify. My honor system was backwards. When other kids were told to go to a policeman if they were in trouble, I was told to never speak to the cops without a lawyer! The people you were taught to trust, I was taught to fear. Yes, you get to an age where you know right from wrong, but when you grow up believing in all the wrong things, it's hard to shake those beliefs!

My oldest brother was out of jail again and with a woman who was so ugly she made onions cry! I'm sorry, I hate to call people ugly, but this woman was a hideous creature inside and out. They were both strung out on heroin and were quickly falling apart. No one could have seen what was coming, but by the time the dust settled my little dysfunctional family would be in tatters. I had just returned to our little apartment. Linda and I had gone to the Social Security building to get her card. I had signed us in, and it's a good thing I did—but more on that later. I noticed my neighbor looking at me funny, but I brushed it off as I approached my door. This was long before cell phones or pagers. There was a note in bold letters, "Fred, go home. Your father has been shot!"

## Chapter 7
### Permanent Vacation

The world was spinning under my feet. I could hardly comprehend the words on the page. I ran outside and jumped in a cab. I had a million questions buzzing through my brain, but the most prevalent was, "Is my father alive?"

I pulled up across the street, threw money at the cabbie and stepped out. A reporter from Channel 11 news was in my face. "Do you know who shot your father?"

I was angry about the intrusion and said something like, "Lady, I just got here." I hurried across the street and ducked under the yellow tape. As I moved toward my father's house, three police were on me, blocking my path and asking me to raise my hands. I was asking questions, and they weren't answering. Finally I said "What the fuck are you searching me for? Where's my father? IS HE DEAD?"

"Yes, Fred, your father is dead. Is there somewhere you can go to collect yourself?"

I walked away with questions bursting in my mind like fireworks. "Who did this? Where's my mother? How long ago? Is anyone in custody?"

I ask a cop standing outside these questions, which he ignored!

I was standing there trying to process this information when a reporter walked up and asked if they could ask some questions. I mumbled some kind of answer, and she started to ask the usual reporter questions. I mumbled some incoherent answers and the questions never did make the news. At this time, my mother pulled up, flanked by two lawyers. As I approached, the lawyer yelled at me for speaking to the press. "Don't say a fuckin' word without me present!"

I didn't have the capacity to put up a argument, I simply looked at my mom and said, "Who did this?"

The lawyer answered for her. "Come on, Fred. You know Johnny did this."

I looked to my mother trying to read her face, but there was nothing there. Besides, she had those big Joan Crawford sunglasses on, so it was hard to tell!

My father's body had already been removed and slowly the crime lab people left, then the uniformed police started peeling off, then finally the detectives walked over. "We will be by tomorrow. We will have more questions" I guess I was numb, but my mother and I sat in the living room as the house cleared out. We were a few feet from where my father drew his last breath a few hours before. There was a huge bloodstain on the carpet and blood splatter on the refrigerator—as well as pieces of my father's brain. I tried to get answers from my mother, but I figured she was in shock, so I set about cleaning up the best I could. It's very hard to clean up the blood of someone you love; I hope none of you ever face that situation. For those of you who have, you know exactly what I mean.

As darkness fell on August 5$^{th}$, 1988, I had a head full of questions, a dead father, a mother who wasn't speaking, a pregnant girlfriend at home, and my oldest brother nowhere to be found. The door opened and in walked my sister, who now lived in Delaware. She was on vacation with her husband and son when she got the call. She drove from the Jersey Shore to Baltimore in a few hours. I'll never know how fast she must have been driving, but she apparently raced down the highway. She walked in and had questions. She wasn't backing off, just started firing questions at my mother. Cindy had become a tough, no-nonsense woman. She had made her peace with our father and forgiven him for the terrible things he had done to her as a little girl. I overheard a conversation where he had called her crying, begging her for forgiveness. She had completely forgiven him, which speaks to her incredible strength. She would later tell me she knew our father was a sick man and that when he got older, he was truly sorry for the things he did to us kids.

On this night F. Lee Bailey would have been proud of Cindy's cross-examination of our mother. One of Mom's stories was she came home from a Dr.'s appointment to find my father on the floor dead. The next one had her just getting home from a Dr.'s appointment when my oldest brother came to the door. My father let him in, and John asked to use the bathroom. He was taking a long time, so my mother started up the stairs. John rushed past my mom, coming down the steps. By the time she got turned around, she heard three pops and came down to find John running out the door and my father on the floor with three gunshot wounds!

Only my mother, John and my father knew exactly what took place in those few moments, but here are the facts as gleaned from three murder trials, police reports and eyewitness accounts.

My father was drinking more than usual. He had fallen off the wagon and was being really nasty. He had been diagnosed with prostate cancer, and it was a hard hit for him. This was a man who had a wife and two or three girlfriends at any given time. I think his plumbing problems made him all the more angry, and when he drank, he turned into the monster from my childhood. He took to wearing a robe around the house, and his paranoia had him venturing out less than usual. Between his illnesses—both mental and physical—and his drinking, he started making mistakes. My father had countless run-ins with the law and had done minimal time. To say he was careful is to say an eel is kinda slippery. A couple days before his murder, I stopped by the house to find him drunk in bed at 3:30 in the afternoon. As I waited for him to collect himself, I stood in the kitchen drinking an iced tea. I heard him coming and looked up to see him pointing his .38 Special at me. He fired, and the bullet missed by inches, slamming into the door. I ran out to a waiting car, stopping to throw my glass at his house. He answered by shooting through the plate glass window that had been replaced more then I can keep count. I jumped in the car and went home. I would later wonder what life would have been like if he had put that gun away in the safe, but he slid it under his mattress and passed out.

I called home the next day. My father picked up the phone and started talking as if nothing had happened between us. He began telling me about a fight between him and some guy who was in a bar talking about robbing him. The truth is, the guy didn't fight back. He was a neighborhood guy who got drunk and was talking to hear the sound of his own voice. I saw the guy in prison a few years later, and besides giving me a terrible haircut, he was a harmless type of guy—only dangerous with scissors! At any rate, I listened to my father ramble on that morning, not knowing it would be the last time I'd hear his voice.

The next morning, around 9:30 a.m., a guy named John Norris stopped by the house to buy pills from my father. He was there a few minutes. My mother was in the front room folding clothes. As Norris left, my oldest brother passed by him, headed toward my father's back door. John Norris later testified that as he started his van, he heard three snapping sounds as he pulled off. He looked toward the house and saw no activity, so he headed home to get high.

The next-door neighbor mixed up his days and told the police that he witnessed me running from the house. No wonder the cops were patting me down when I showed up. The detectives later found out I was signed in to a government building twenty miles away!

Another witness said my mother almost ran him over pulling out of the yard at around 9:50 a.m. My lifelong "friend," who lived across the street, went to the local precinct and asked to speak to detectives. He told them that something wasn't right about The Greek's murder, and it was probably Johnny, Marie (my mother) and Freddie who killed him. It was madness. It seemed that everyone wanted to make a statement, speak with detectives or talk to reporters. It seems I was the only one confused; everybody else knew "exactly" what happened!

It was an ugly, messed-up time. I had to take care of my mother and make funeral arrangements. I had a million thoughts running through my head when I went upstairs and found my father's pills in his open safe. The cops left them there because they were my Mom's prescription meds. I crushed three of them and shot up while my mother and sister talked downstairs. As I walked down the steps, the hydromorphone clouding my brain, a knock came at the door. I opened it, and there stood John Lacey!

Chapter 8
Screaming in the Night

"Where's Mommy?" he said in the Southern drawl he had developed in a Carolina prison.

I looked over my shoulder to see Cindy headed toward us "Let him in!" she barked. If there was any fear of him, she wasn't showing it. As for me, I must admit I was a bit nervous. He never liked me, and now there was nothing in his way. My sister looked him square in the eye "You killed Daddy?" It was a bit of a question and a lot of an accusation.

"I don't know what the hell you're talking about. I came to talk to Mommy!"

John leered at Cindy as Cindy sat down next to our mother. "So talk." Cindy knew exactly what John wanted: he wanted money, pills or both, and she knew he wouldn't ask in front of her. My mother was visibly shaken. She and John had the most uncomfortable ten minutes or so of conversation a mother and son can have. He soon left, leaving a heavy silence in the room, broken finally by Cindy looking our mother in the eye and saying, "I know he killed Daddy."

The question hanging in the air, one that would never be answered, was—did our mother tell him to do it? We would never hear an answer, and it's still heatedly debated around holiday dinners. On this night, it was time for someone to take some kind of action. We decided Mom would come to my apartment, and Cindy would head home to take care of her young son and husband. The next day, I got up early to call funeral homes and started preparing for the funeral. I just about had everything nailed down when a knock came at my door. I tucked a .38 snub nose in my belt and answered the door. There stood John Lacey and his wildebeest-looking girlfriend.

"I'm not here for trouble. Can I see Mom?" I let him in, and he started talking. "I guess you know by now I'm the one who killed the old man." The statement hit me with the force of a sledgehammer. He continued to talk, but I didn't hear the words. I contemplated pulling my gun and emptying it into his ugly face. By the time I started hearing his words again, he said, "I need some money to get out of town, and I'm dope sick."

I can't describe the war that raged inside my head. I barely said a word as my mother gave him some pills and a few hundred dollars. As he headed for the door, he said, "Fred, I know you have some guns around here. Let me hold one. I can't go back inside. I'd rather take myself out before I'll go back."

I looked at him, not believing my ears. "Do you expect me to hand you a loaded gun, John?" I said incredulously.

"I promise I won't do nothing to you. I just can't do any more time." I have to admit the thought of him killing himself appealed to me. I went in the bedroom of my small apartment and took a small .25 automatic out of my chest of drawers. I took the clip out and removed the bullets, then slammed the clip back in the gun!

I had a plan of sorts, I would hand him the gun, and if he pointed it at me, I would grab my gun and unload in him. Surely, I could say it was self-defense. I was in my own apartment, and he had killed my father the day before. I walked back out to my living room where he and Bigfoot stood by the door. I took a breath and handed him the .25 automatic. He immediately tucked it in his waist and opened the door. He made it to his girlfriend's car when I caught up to him and handed him the bullets for the .25. A certain part wanted him to pull that gun on me. I was scared, I admit, but that guy will never know how close he came to dying that day. He pulled away, and I don't know how I felt. Relieved? Cheated? Nauseated? Maybe all of the above! I flipped a cigarette and walked back in my apartment.

No sooner then I shut the door I heard a knock. I just knew Lacey had come back to kill me with my own gun! I pulled my .38. When a voice came through the door, "Fred, it's Detective Wilson; I have a few questions," I put my gun under the seat cushion and opened the door. There stood Detectives Wilson and Flanagan , I've changed their names like I have many others in this book, but these were two very professional men who, I must say, I have a great deal of respect for. "Can you walk out to the car?"

I mumbled my consent and followed them. Here I was about to be interviewed by two guys I know are much smarter than me. All my life I had been taught never to rat on someone, the cops were the bad guys, and always ask for a lawyer, but another part of me wanted my brother held accountable for his terrible actions. I loved my father, but he wasn't a great father. In fact, he was a terrible father, but he was the only father I had! To say I was confused would be an understatement of epic proportions.

These cops knew exactly who they were dealing with. They slow rolled me and made me comfortable, even making some jokes about police procedure. It wasn't long before I was telling them that my brother had admitted to killing my father. They asked if I knew where he was. I honestly didn't at that moment. Then they hit me with a question I had asked myself a thousand times in the last 24 hours, but never out loud. "Fred, do you think your mother had anything to do with your father's murder?"

The words echoed in my brain; my breath caught in my throat. I relaxed and released my breath. I relied on years of training as I looked directly into the detective's eyes and lied, "Absolutely not."

They thanked me for my time and started to leave. "One more thing, Fred. Do you think we could stop by the house later? We want to look at the carpet where your father was found."

I knew instantly why they wanted that—they wanted to know how long my father laid there before the 911 call went out. "Sorry, guys, I cut it out and threw it away. Blood is too hard to clean." As they left, I knew I had to get to the house and get rid of that carpet.

I was a street-smart kid, and the cops had let me know what they were doing by the flow of their questions. As I walked away from that conversation, I had a picture of things to come. They knew John pulled the trigger. He was a dumbo, and surely they could pick him up at anytime and gather enough evidence to send him away for a few more decades. But if they were building a case against my mother, they knew they had an uphill battle. It wasn't going to be easy to hang a murder on a sick old lady who suffered years of abuse at her husband's hands. A conspiracy isn't the easiest thing to prove, but they intended to try. I walked away with that knowledge, but I had so many things to do, first of which, was to head to the bathroom and shoot enough hydromorphone to kill a horse. After a tumbler of Smirnoff, I got on the phone making funeral arraignments for my father, who was in a coroner's office with three .38 Special holes in his head. The report that came out at trial said the first bullet entered the lower backside of his head and exited through his forehead; the second went in the left side of his head and exited his right temple; and the last shot was after he hit the floor. It went through his right cheek, out his left and into the carpet. It was indeed a vicious, cold-blooded execution!

Chapter 9
Screaming for Vengeance

Drug abuse is never good, but I swear it held me together over the next few days. My mother had 30k in a purse at my apartment. I used some of it to pay for my father's funeral. On the first day of the viewing, we got there a little early. We had about an hour before people would start showing up. I went into the bathroom and injected some Dilaudid. I had put the syringe in my sock and was dabbing blood from my arm when the door slammed open and there stood a uniformed police officer, gun in hand. "Where's your mother?" he demanded.

Before I could answer, one of the cops yelled to him "We got her!"

The cop looked at me. "Put your fuckin' hands up and be a good boy," he snarled. He led me out of the bathroom and put me on my knees in the lobby of the funeral home as two plain clothes cops and a handful of uniformed cops led my mother out in cuffs. One cop took pity on my mother and put a towel over her head so the reporters wouldn't see a crying old lady being led from her husband's viewing in cuffs.

In a few moments, they were gone, and I was still on my knees. The cop had put his gun away as I got to my feet. "Sorry, Freddie. We knew you'd be upset, and we were just trying to prevent anyone from getting hurt." I looked back at him blankly as he turned to leave. I stood there, my world in shambles and my brain in overdrive. I was trying to think of what to do next, but rational thought escaped me. As I waited for my mother to see a commissioner to set her bail, I got on the phone to the bail bondsman we used all the time to tell him my mother had been arrested. I wanted her out as soon as a bail was set. He knew I was serious and got to work. I called the lawyer and left a message. That was all the action I could take. Now I just had to wait, and believe me, sometimes just waiting is a very difficult thing to do. So I went back to the bathroom to inject more drugs. Man, I was a messed-up kid!

A handful of people knew what happened, but most who showed up that first night had no idea my mother was arrested. I was meeting and greeting and accepting condolences, and my mind was elsewhere. I had a preacher come in to speak to the crowd. As the preacher was standing there looking at me, I was looking at him, waiting for him to step up to the podium and do his thing. Finally, I said, "Excuse me, sir, are you going to speak?"

He looked at me and said, "Well, I hate to bring it up, but your mother was supposed to make a donation to the church."

I couldn't believe it. I had all these things going on, and I'm being shook down by a preacher. I turned away from him and stepped up to the podium myself. I figured I got more right to speak then this donation-seeking suit! I don't recall the things I said, but people came up to me afterward and were patting me on the back. I even managed to work things out with the preacher, who agreed to show up on the day of burial to officiate... for a seventy-five dollar donation. I was starting to believe I could get through this when I looked up, and there was John Lacey coming through the door, drunk as the day is long.

He was a total mess, crying all over the place and telling anyone who would listen that "The Greek was a helluva man!" He put a bottle of whiskey in the coffin, which someone quickly removed. I finally pulled him to the side and told him the police were looking for him. I gave him a hundred dollars and a few pills and told him to leave before they came back to get him. He told me where he was going and slobbered for a few minutes about how he loved "The Greek." I assured him that Daddy forgave him, and that he had to go because it's what dad would have wanted. Truth be told, I would have told him anything to get him out of that funeral home. After I absolved him of his sins, he seemed OK as he stumbled toward the exit still blubbering about what a great man our father was. As he left, I let out a sigh of relief. Everybody around me was giving me credit for handling so many things so well. I never did admit it was the pharmaceuticals that were seeing me through. I felt like such a coward.

I stepped outside to light a cigarette. As I took a deep pull off of my Newport, I heard a door open. It was a lifelong friend of the family. "Fred, it's the detective on the phone. He wants to speak to you."

I just looked at her for a moment. "Tell him I'll be there in a minute." I took another drag as she disappeared back inside. I was in no hurry to talk to these jerks; they locked my mother up while John's out getting drunk. I took my time before walking into the funeral home and to the lobby where half a dozen people stood around a phone waiting to eavesdrop on my conversation. I picked up the phone, which had a long cord and headed toward the bathroom.

The detective spoke to me in that 'I'm your buddy' tone that they practice to disarm people in the interrogation room. "Freddie, I know you're upset over us arresting your mom, but she will never go to trial. We only picked her up to get her to tell us the truth about John! She has cooperated and will be released in the morning, but we need to pick up John. After all, if he finds out she cooperated, well..." He allowed my imagination to paint a picture far uglier than his words could have conveyed.

He had lied about nearly everything, of course. The only truth in the detective's words were that they wanted to arrest John. I told them where John was. I didn't have an address, so I had to give them detailed directions to my cousin's house where John had said he was going earlier in the evening. The cops went there and my cousin admitted to getting them a motel room at a cheap little place out on Rt. 40. The kinda spot the hookers kept regular rooms in. The detective got a pass key from the manager, and they approached the room with guns drawn. John was inside fast asleep next to his girlfriend when they opened the door and pounced on him. There was the .25 automatic on the nightstand next to him, but he never had a chance to get it. In seconds, these trained officers had him on his face handcuffed. I'm very happy no one got hurt with the .25 automatic I gave him!

Two days later, I took the tax papers down to the courthouse so my mother could post her house against the fifty thousand bail they had given her. I now knew the detectives lied to me; the charges against my mother remained, but I was happy to have her out. It terrified me to think of my sick old mother in jail with real criminals! She came to my apartment and picked up her money. She had missed my father's funeral, but if she was upset, she showed no outward signs. She told me she was going to stay with my sister in New Jersey for awhile. Without a word of thanks or anything, she left. I silently kicked myself for not stealing a few hundred dollars, but I had some pills left. My mother would be getting her new prescription before she left for the Garden State. It was a terrible time. I had never seen my mother so quiet and really didn't know what to believe.

When she got to Cindy's house, my sister told my mother how I handled everything from the viewing and funeral to the lawyers, bail bondsman and tax papers and everything in between. Cindy explained she couldn't get time off, but took a personal day to come to the funeral, and that I had done an awesome job. The next day, a Fed Ex guy showed up and handed me a large, thick envelope from my mother. Inside was one thousand dollars, and man did I need it.

I was at my father's house the next day doing general cleanup and collecting the mail and such when a friend of my father's stopped by. He was looking for some Dilaudid and asked me if I could sell him a few. I had a few left, but I didn't want to part with them. I didn't know when I could get some more, and I had managed to get a small habit in the past week or so. I really didn't know what having a habit was, but I sure was getting ready to find out. When my father's friend said, "Damn, man, I hate to have to go into town," I jumped on it.

"Do you know someone with Dilaudid in the city?" I asked quickly.

He smiled. "No, man, but I can get some really good dope." This was to be an introduction from hell. I had no idea what I was getting into, but I would soon find myself in a brand new world, full of new people, new highs, and new lows so low that I can barely believe I lived through it!!

## Chapter 10
## Highway to Hell

I could blame the guy who introduced me to heroin, but the truth is, I took to it like a fish to water. From the first taste I knew I had found my true love, and yes, horror would follow, but it starts out like a beautiful lullaby. If it started out bad, no one would end up addicted (and unfortunately, the number of people dependent on the drug is staggering). At the time, in the late '80s, you had to go into the black neighborhood to get it. Most white guys would get ripped off, or worse. I learned the game thing quick. I started buying $60 wax bags of the white powder. It was a kind of heroin they call "scramble"—it's heroin mixed with Benita and quianide, and it comes in many strengths. My first overdose came about a month after I started using it.

I was out with a dancer. Her name was Tina, and she danced at a bar called Haven Place. It was about 4:00 a.m. when we got to her house on a notorious little street called Yorkway. I had four $60 bags of heroin. We quickly split a bag and headed for the bedroom. Sex is incredible on heroin. I'll leave the details to your imagination, but it gives you sexual endurance and heightens all your senses! We took a break, and I sent her to the kitchen to get me something to drink. I was smart enough to put my money and dope in my shoes. She wasn't my first dancer, but when she took too long to come back, I looked down and saw my pants gone. I walked out and snatched the jeans she was searching out of her hands. I put them on, along with the rest of my clothes, listening to her tell me how she wasn't robbing me and we should do a little more dope and she would "make me see God" and all those things I'd heard more than once before!

I quickly drove to my father's house since it was closer then my apartment. I had a friend of the family staying there while my mother stayed with my sister. If he had known there was sixty thousand dollars in cash over his head hidden in the drop ceiling, he would have had one hell of a party. I opened the door and scared the hell out of him. I rushed past him, grabbing a spoon as I headed toward the bathroom. I really don't know what I was thinking, but I dumped a huge amount of heroin onto a soup spoon, poured almost a full syringe worth of water on it, put fire under the spoon and brought the liquid to a boil. At last the milky water began to clear. After I had it properly cooked, I took a five-dollar glassine bottle of cocaine, twisted the red top off and dumped the coke in to mix with my heroin. This is a speedball, and its killed many people, including John Belushi and Chris Farley, to name a couple. I injected the substance into my arm.

As the wave of coke hit me, I knew I was in trouble. I started down the steps, my vision closing in as the ringing in my ears kept growing, and made it to the bottom step before I hit the ground. The world was spinning wildly as I lost consciousness.

I saw no light at the end of a tunnel. I saw blackness, and as I drifted into the abyss of that blackness, I felt no fear—just a quiet peace. I was perfectly content there in my nothingness, just floating around when I heard a voice.

"We got a pulse! Can you believe it? This fuckin' kid is alive! Hit him with more Narcon."

I opened my eyes. A lady was standing over me. She brushed my hair back and said "That good feeling is about to leave you." I smiled in my narcotic haze. I can remember thinking I'd like to sleep with her, then a feeling hit me. I sat straight up in the bed. It was the worst feeling ever. It was like going into withdrawal at five hundred miles an hour! Every nerve stood at attention and screamed. I was in such pain; I couldn't stand it as I screamed for them to stop, but it was too late. The Narcon running through my veins catapulted me into instant and severe withdrawal, a feeling nearly impossible to describe, but it feels like every nerve is on fire. You have a million bugs on you and a million snakes in you; your muscles cramp and your bowels loosen. It's a pain like you've never felt, and they don't feel sorry for you because you put yourself in that situation.

I tried to get up, but there was a tube in my penis and needles in my arm. "Just relax for five minutes, and we will take them out." Ten minutes later I was walking out of the hospital. I hopped in a cab and said, "Pennsylvania and Gold." The cabbie looked at me like I was crazy. If it hadn't been 10:00 a.m., I'm sure he wouldn't have taken me, but I threw a fifty dollar bill at him and he stepped on the gas. Within an hour, I copped more heroin and was shooting it in the back of the cab, having bought a syringe on the same corner where I bought the dope.

I got back to my father's house. He had been dead for more than six weeks, but I still saw it as 'my father's house.' I jumped in the shower and got some clean clothes on. "Hey, David, did Linda call?

"Yes, she did, about thirty times!" he said, a little more exasperated than I liked, but the guy did save my life by calling me an ambulance, so I let it slide.

I picked up the phone. "Hey, Linda, I'll be there in a

few hours. I gotta do a thing." I always have said that and still do. It means I'm doing something. Don't ask what it is because all I'm going to say is 'it's a thing.'" My wife doesn't like it these days, but I like to feel like I'm a man of mystery and she allows it... sometimes. Anyway, Linda said she had been having pains all night. Before she finished the sentence, I was headed home.

Look, I won't lie; I was a terrible boyfriend. I didn't love her, and I ran around like I was single. I was immersed in the drug life. I wanted wild dancers, not the girl next door. I was raised around people who had a wife and a girlfriend, and I thought no more about having women on the side then I did going to get a pack of smokes. However, I loved the little boy that was growing in my girlfriend's belly, and the day he was born was the happiest day of my life. I swore off drugs, and I swore off extra girlfriends (an occasional blowjob would be OK). I was gonna be a good father. I was going to get a real job and be all the things my father wasn't. I was pretty good for about two weeks, and when I say pretty good, I mean I was taking Percocet for the heroin withdrawal and I was still drinking and taking Valium at night so I could sleep. It all came to a head one night when I went to a bar called Mr. Bees. It was a packaged goods place and bar. I went to get a twelve pack of beer, and as I stepped out of my car, I saw this blonde with white, skin-tight jeans walking toward the door of the bar. She had big, '80s platinum hair with blue eye shadow and six-inch stilettos to match. She knew I was looking, and she started throwing her hips. As she opened the bar door, I heard Rockin' Rod singing *Hot Legs* from the jukebox. I followed her in. I didn't go home for three days. The blonde was incredible fun, but as I promised her I'd call, we both knew I was lying. Still, little did I know what was waiting for me when I got home!

Chapter 11
Dope Man, Dope Man

As I reached for the doorknob, I knew something was wrong. It was locked. It was never locked! I fished my key out and slid it in the lock. I swung open the door, and the small interior looked absolutely cavernous. I even thought I heard an echo when I called Linda's name. She wasn't there. Neither was my furniture or anything else. Well, she did leave the bed in the bedroom and my clothes, too. I can't say I was all that surprised. It was just a matter of time before she got tired of putting up with my lifestyle choices. I never figured I'd care if she left, and the truth is, I didn't care that she was gone, but I did care about my son being gone.

OK, obviously she had been planning this for some time, so I knew she was back in New York. I got on the phone to her mother. Her mother lied to me and said she hadn't heard from her, but my son tipped me off by crying in the background. I headed for New York within the hour. I knew it wasn't time to use threats; I'd only do that if she forced my hand. No, it was time for Mr. Lover! I picked up some heroin for the trip and headed north on I-95. As I got into New York, I bought some flowers from some guy at a stoplight and headed to Linda's mother's house. Linda opened the door, and I saw the fear in her eyes. "Hey, take it easy. I drove a long way to see the girl I wanna marry." Her face relaxed, and she opened the door. I gave her the flowers and leaned in to give her my most gentle kiss! We sat at the kitchen table and talked. I told her how sorry I was and how I came to my senses when I saw that empty apartment. It was getting late and I knew she was loving all the attention I was giving her, so I asked if I could stay the night. She agreed immediately, and we headed for the bedroom

    I took my time hitting all the right buttons, saying all the right things and moving very slow. As she drifted off to sleep, I was pretty satisfied with myself. I got up and watched my son sleep. It felt good knowing he'd be back home in a day or two. The next morning, we talked it over. I would head back and get things set up at the apartment. I'd wire money, then Linda and my son would get on a Greyhound and come home.

    I got home and called one of my favorite girls. She was a curvy Mexican girl named Rosalita. I gave her a few hundred dollars and told her to fix my apartment up perfectly for Linda's return. She did an awesome job, and the apartment looked great. I called Linda, who sounded incredibly excited when I told her how lovely the apartment looked. She asked me to wire her money to come home and to send extra so she could give her mom some money. I wired $500 and waited for my son to be back home. I waited and waited and waited. The realization that I had been worked out of my money dawned slowly and turned to fury over the next 24 hours. I drove back to New York. It was a wasted trip. The house was empty. Some neighbors said they left for Arizona, while others said Colorado.

    As I drove home, the thought that I would never see my son again hit me, and I began to cry. I thought about my father and the tears came even harder. The thought that I would always be alone terrified me. I needed some drugs and a warm body to curl up with. When I got home, I got both. I picked up some dope and coke and called Rose. I told her what happened, and she said she knew just what I needed. When she showed up at my apartment an hour later with a blonde in a leather dress, I welcomed the distraction. We partied all night. They left in the morning, and I laid in the bed feeling miserable. How did my life get so bad? What was I doing wrong? The good news is things couldn't get any worse, could they? I was about to find out, and I wasn't going to like the answer!

It was a few nights later. I was drunk and hanging with an acquaintance when I got the bright idea to do a storehouse breaking and entering, I have no idea what I was thinking. I really didn't need the money. I was just drunk and disgusted with my life and just out of my mind. I went through the roof of the gun shop with a hammer. I had no plan, other than steal some guns and get out of there. I hit the display case right away, which is a big mistake, I'm not writing a blueprint for robbery, so let's just say I made many mistakes, starting with entering the place at all. I ran outside with a duffel bag full of guns, but my ride had left me. I started running. I cut through a yard and ran right into a responding officer. The only smart thing I did was put my arms in the air and allow the officer to take the duffel bag and pistols from my waist. They didn't beat me up or treat me badly, and I went to jail without a fight. The cop laughed at me and gave me a cigarette. I got a seventy-five thousand dollar bail that got dropped to twenty-five thousand at bail review. I was home within a week. I had charges pending, and my dope habit went into high gear.

I let the apartment go. I was spending more time in the city closer to my drug. I fit in perfectly, even though I was the only white guy on Chase Street in East Baltimore. My mother was back and forth between my sister's house and my father's house. She was working on her case with the lawyers. Things were getting really bad for me. I was strung to the gills by the time my court case came up. I tried to postpone it, but the judge wasn't having it. I really believed I would get probation. After all, I always did when my father was alive. Boy, was I surprised when the judge handed down five years. He suspended two-and-a-half years of it and sent me to prison that day. The withdrawal was so intense they actually put me in the infirmary at the prison. I can't tell you how sick you have to be to get medicated in jail, but they gave me medicine for the withdrawal. I was released from the infirmary to gen pop in about a week, I was still sick as a dog and, believe it or not, the older cons had mercy on me. One old man gave me all his oranges, which was all I could keep down.

When you go into DOC in Maryland, you are sent to a building called Maryland Reception Diagnostic and Classification Center, but everyone just calls it Diagnostics or DOC. While you're there, they classify you and decide what jail you do you time in. They use a number system that goes by many factors, such as length of sentence, nature of crime, general attitude and things along those lines. This was my first sentence with the big boys, so they made me minimum security. However, my luck was still in the dumps. At least that was my view at the time, but looking back on my life I can see where God protected me with each step. They had no room at the minimum security prisons, so I was sent to medium security pending placement in the minimum section. Confused yet? Well, imagine being there. It's not like the movies, but in some ways it is. There was no band of roving homosexuals just waiting to pounce like in the movies, but there are people who want to take advantage of you at every turn. It's just the tactics are a little more subtle at first.

I was sent to a place called 'The New Jail' in

Hagerstown, MD. Hagerstown is a small farming community about an hour and a half outside Baltimore. It has two major employment opportunities—farming and prisons! MCI-H (that's the old jail that looks like a castle) was built by prisoners. A lot of old-timers call it "The Farm" because in the early days of the prison, it was, in fact, a working farm. That era was long gone, and it was now a high/medium security prison, reserved for hard heads and those with big time. Next to that was M.C.T.C., the Maryland Correctional Training Center, or The New Jail, as it was known. If it weren't for the rolled barbed wire, you'd think it was a college, at least from the outside. Down the street from those prisons was the newest jai. It was called R.C.I., or Roxbury Correctional Center, which was just called Roxbury since M.C.T.C. would always be known as The New Jail.

The hour-and-a-half drive from diagnostics to M.C.T.C. is actually a six-hour trip because they stop at the Jessup institutions on the way, I was handcuffed and shackled for the trip with a chain around my waist and my handcuffs connected to it with a black box that prevented movement and the possibility of tampering with the restraints. The chain around your waist was locked with a standard lock. I could hardly believe all the steel I was wrapped in, but the transportation officer tried to lighten the mood by asking me if I liked heavy metal. By the time I got to The New Jail, I was wrung out. The trip was long and hot and when we got there, I was pulled off the bus and pushed into a dog cage. They gave me warm milk and two sandwiches. I would say it was bologna, but no one was really sure what it was.

Housing Unit 6 is for new guys. I was put in 6a in a single cell within an hour! When I looked out at the rolling barbed wire, my tough guy persona hit the wall. I looked up to the sky and said out loud, "Freddie, what did you get yourself into this time?" Tears welled up in my eyes and flowed like a river. I was scared and alone in a man's prison, and my brother right across the street at the old jail couldn't help me. In fact, he would try to hurt me. He always was an asshole, but prison had made him bitter. He believed I owed him something. He should have tried to protect me, but he didn't, a slight I'll never forget. I had to make my own way through this prison bit and after the tears, I washed my face and resolved to make it by any means necessary. I wasn't going to be anyone's bitch; I was going to make it through with my own name.

    I made it through, alright, but more trouble was brewing.

Chapter 12
No Parole from Rock and Roll

The New Jail isn't like the show *Oz,* but make no mistake—it's a medium sec prison that houses some dangerous men. I was waiting on my transfer to the Quonset Huts, which is a minimum security jail within the jail (I'm sure you follow). I would have my first prison run-in not with the Aryan Brotherhood or some notorious prison gang. No, it came from a guy my brother put on me. My brother Steve was angry over some seriously stupid stuff. Some junkie girl was coming to see him, and he wrote me to ask what she was up to out there on the streets. Well, he didn't like my answer! He sent a letter to a guy he knew who had been at the old jail with him and told him to lean on me. I heard this guy was looking to see me and to be honest, I found it wildly amusing. I mean, I know my family is messed up, but this is low even for my brother! I saw the guy on the way to commissary. Someone tipped me off and as soon as he approached, I swung. It caught him completely by surprise, which was good for me. I stunned him. He thought he was gonna put his finger in my face, call me a bitch and walk away.

It got broken up fast, and I gained a quick reputation for swing now, talk later. My reaction was out of fear, but it worked for me. In a week or so, I got moved to the huts and had a little fight my first week there. At the time I thought I was gonna have to be fighting all the time. However, it wasn't like that. I made it known I wasn't a pushover. I wouldn't let you take my stuff, and I wouldn't be disrespected. I thought I knew prison, but this was the tip of the iceberg, so to speak. I made it through just reading books and educating myself. Older cons who saw me at the books encouraged me and even tutored me. I took a paralegal course just for the knowledge! I stayed out of the drama of daily prison life. I learned the rules quickly. Don't borrow anything, don't accept gifts, the TV in the recall isn't your and don't walk on those hillbilly's grass! I must touch on this subject for a moment because those Hagerstown guards are their own breed!

I was never a racist dude. I like black music, I love black women and racism wasn't an issue growing up! I dealt with a lot of black people when I got into heroin, and I never have seen any percentage in hating anyone simply because of color. Now those Hagerstown guards are like something out of a movie. They still call black men "boy" and throw "nigger" around like the word has no bad meaning at all. Ninety-nine percent of the guards in Hagerstown prisons are white males, and the only thing they hate worse than a "nigger" is a "nigger lover"! In my first week, I had a visit from a beautiful mulatto girl I met in Baltimore. She was the sister of a guy I bought heroin from. We had gone out a few times, but she was a good girl, so I really didn't pursue her hard, 'cause I didn't want to drag her down. She came to see me and told me if I stayed off the junk when I got out, that maybe we could have a future. I made all the promises, and she came to see me by bus once a month. Man, I wonder what my life would have been if I had done right and married her, but I'll never know.

Anyway, on her first visit, I was so happy to see her. You're allowed to kiss at the beginning and end of the visit. I was starved for affection, and I took advantage of that first embrace. When I had walked in, there was one guard working the visiting room. When he yelled at me for kissing too long, I looked over and five guards were staring at me. I thought they were checking out my visitor 'cause she was so beautiful; boy, was I wrong! After the visit, about ten of us went back to our housing unit and I was the only one to get strip searched! The guards were standing around talking about my visitor like she was a piece of trash. "Hey, nigger lover, that nigger girl like it in her ass?" one of them said in a Southern drawl.

"I didn't know baboons liked little white dicks," another hillbilly added. My face was red with fury and they knew they were getting to me, and they kept it up saying some of the meanest things they could think of, and all I could do was take it. If I had opened my mouth, they would have beaten me senseless.

As I walked across the compound back to the area known as the huts, I stepped on the grass. My foot barely touched a blade as I was getting out of the way of guys running over to the gym. A big hillbilly called out, "Hey, boy, come 'ere." As I walked toward the big guard, I knew I was in trouble, I didn't know why, but I knew by the look on his face, he was about 6 foot 6 and a good three hundred pounds. The closer I got, the bigger he got. "Look at me nigger lover. You see that asphalt? That's where your ass walk!"

I was stunned by his words. My foot had barely touched the grass. I was about sick of this treatment, all because I wasn't a redneck. "Look, officer, I..." He back-handed me with a hand that felt like it was made of iron. It knocked me off my feet and dazed the hell out of me. "Get up," he ordered, and I got up, albeit a little wobbly.

"You got something to say, nigger lover?" I shook my head no and walked back to my housing area feeling less than human.

I knuckled down and stayed to myself, reading and working out. Time started flying. I made parole after six months, but they gave me a seven-month delayed release. I missed John's trial. He pled guilty to second degree murder and was sentenced to thirty years for killing my father. My mother's trial lasted three days and ended in a hung jury, meaning twelve men and women couldn't decide if she was guilty. When this happens, the prosecution can either drop the case or try it again. They chose to try it a second time, but my mother's case wouldn't go to trial for two more years while her lawyers argued double jeopardy. As the legal arguments stretched out, my
mother's bank account dwindled.

I was released on May 2, 1990, with the plan to stay away from drugs and crime altogether. What I missed most in prison was sex, and that was all I had on my mind. A family friend picked me up and drove me back to my father's house. My mother was living back home full-time, but she just didn't look well. I figured the stress of the trial had weighed her down. She had a dead husband and three boys in prison, so life wasn't good for her. She was selling her pills, but people were taking advantage of her left and right. I was home now, and I was going to fix everything. I was going to take care of Mom and pay her bills and get the buyers in line. I never could have dreamt what was really wrong with my mother, but I was soon to find out!!

## Chapter 13
## Little Piggies

I was free, I was sober, and it should have been a great time in my life. I would find out that while I was away, not only had the junkie girl who was going to see my brother been living in my father's house on and off, she had introduced my mother to skin-popping Dilaudid and heroin. I couldn't believe it—my mom had a dope habit at the age of 60!! I mean, she had always taken too many pills, but this was a long way from upping your Percocet dose. She was actually sticking a needle in her arm. She wasn't mainlining but it's hard to argue semantics when your dear old mom is hooked on smack!

It was terrible. I had walked into a powder keg. I had two-and-a-half years to back up if I violated my parole, and on my second day home I was shooting dope! My mother had paid a lot of money to the lawyers, and she had pissed through the rest. Not to mention those who took advantage of her while I was in jail. There wasn't much money left and mom was living on credit cards and what was left from my father. She would end up putting the house in my brother's name and then mine, which would end is disaster… but more on that later.

As news filtered out that I was out of jail, friends

started stopping by to say hi. A girl I'll call Doris ran straight to my house. It was good to see her. Like I said, I had missed sex the most and intended to do my level best to make up for lost time. Freedom was great, but looking back, I was destined to go back to jail the day they released me. My lifelong friend, Chris Kline, stopped by to congratulate me on being released. He was doing well, and I know in his heart, he wanted me to succeed, I also know he didn't think that was likely, and he was very right.

Things spun out of control pretty quick, I started seeing the girl who lived across the alley. Her name was Gina. I wasn't particularly attracted to her; she was a plain-Jane type, with a boyfriend in jail and a few kids running around. She was about ten years older than me, and a bit on the skinny side, but what she did have going for her was her love of narcotics, and she gave the best head I had ever had in my young life! It wasn't a bad relationship. I mean, I never believed in love. I figured that was for suckers. But with her fondness of pharmaceuticals and all things fellatio, she served her purpose just fine.

I was home for a month, and things were really bad. I was shooting dope every day. I didn't have a job, a plan or a future. I thought I was tough now that I was an ex-con, but in reality I was a dope addict who was headed for one of three things: jail, institutions or death! In less than a year, I would be standing in front of a judge on a host of drug charges. My life was a series of pain and disappointment, but this was my crowning achievement. There was no more minimum security jails, no more parole, no more breaks! I was headed to the big time, and I would remain there for four-and-a-half years! You have no idea how long a year can be when you're in jail. People hear that a person got five years and they say, "Oh, he'll be out in three." First off, when a judge gives you five years, it means five years. You can get good time, but it's something you can lose. You can also make parole, but if you're back in prison on a violation of your last parole, well, they tend to frown on that. Finally, five years is a long time to be in prison, with the sadistic guards, the homosexuals, the violence and the games cons play—not to mention missing your girl, your family and friends. Prison is a nightmare you can't wake up from, and I would end up there under some stupid circumstances.

I had a guy I knew through mutual friends stop by the house one day and ask me if I had anyone to "bust a script;" that is, had a doctor's prescription tablet and he would write a fraudulent prescription for, say, one hundred Dilaudid. Whoever took it to the pharmacist would get half the pills. I had this girl Shirley I used for such things, but as luck would have it, I couldn't find her that particular day. I decided to do it myself. Well, the guy failed to tell me they had taken it to the pharmacy a few days before and was told to come back, which is a sure sign they are onto you. I asked for the prescription, and I noticed the pharmacist's hands shaking when she handed me the bag, I knew it was over, but I had to play it out! I asked her some stupid questions trying to judge her demeanor, and she was a nervous wreck. I was waiting for the hand to hit my shoulder, but it didn't come. I walked toward the door and out into the sunshine. I took in a deep breath; I knew it was my last breath of freedom for awhile. I looked to my left and saw two guys hang up side-by-side telephones and start toward me. A car screeched to a halt in front of me, and in seconds there was no less than six guns on me with cops in street clothes throwing me on the ground! It wasn't my first time, so I just shut up and let them do their cop thing. Those guys love to yell and call you names. It's because their adrenaline is pumping and they are scared, so they want to scare you and get you off-balance.

These cops were real cowboys who kept their tough

guy turned on high the whole time. It was all the usual stuff—they asked me to snitch to save myself. I promised to wear a wire and bust people, but I never did and never will. I just wanted them to tell the commissioner I was cooperating so I could get a reduced bail. It worked, and I was out in 24 hours. Of course, they would have the last laugh because it would be me standing in front of the judge in a few months while they were out spending the money they stole from low-level dealers. These cops were the worst kind of cops. They stand on this self-righteous attitude like they are ridding the streets of this evil plague, but the truth is that they are worse than the people they lock up. They knock off low-level dealers, but half the dope and most of the money never make it to the evidence room. No, it goes to their boats and their mistress. The whole time they're stealing, they're looking down on the uneducated kid trying to feed his family! I regret my life back then, and I'm so grateful to God for delivering me from active addiction, but the only thing worse than being what I was is being what they are.

I had a parole violation, a probation violation, and a whole rack of drug charges, and my sentences would stack up like this: two-and-a-half years for violation of probation, two-and-a-half years for violation of parole, five years for possession with the intent to distribute CDS, eighteen months on an unrelated theft, three-and-a-half years for conspiracy to possess with intent to distribute, giving me a grand total of fourteen-and-a-half years. They took me in a back room and told me if I pled guilty, I'd get all my time running concurrent inside the five years, and they would drop prescription fraud and a host of other charges. I accepted the deal and went to diagnostics that day to start my five years, but this would be a very different stay for me. I had no way of knowing I was headed to one of the most dangerous jails in the system!

## Chapter 14
## I Fought the Law and the Law Won

I got sent to diagnostics again, but this time I had a parole violation, and they housed violators at a jail called Putuxent, which also happens to be a prison for the criminally insane. Didn't I tell you I was a lucky man? Anyway, the parole violator is the last in line for everything. The way they see it, you had a chance and blew it, so they will get around to you after everyone else. I would be at Putuxent for six months just waiting to get classified. No good time, no work time, just what's known in the system as dead time. The good news is I was able to get my TV while I was there, and they had the best commissary in the system. The girl I was with when I got my time came to the visiting room to tell me she would wait for me and that I was the best man she ever had. She pledged her undying love to me and walked out of the visiting room. I haven't seen her since!!

It was for the best. When you're doing time, your mind has to be right there with you, not thinking about what some woman is doing out in the free world. While I was there, my older brother Steve was up at the old jail participating in riots. They had a situation at his jail where the guys refused to come in from the small yard. They had one representative from each race go talk to the warden about conditions in the jail. Steve represented the white guys. They gave them a bag lunch, put the prison on lockdown and sent each "representative" to a different prison. Steve got sent to MCI-J in Jessup, which is where I was classified to go. I went to my counselor and told him that my brother and me didn't get along, and I didn't want to go to the same jail. My counselor assured me he would take care of it. The next morning they woke me up; I was to be transferred that day. I was being sent to MCI-H, the old jail where my brother had just been transferred from!

When they told me where I was going, my heart jumped to my throat. Even other guys being transferred to other jails asked me who I pissed off. It was well known that the old jail was one of the worst prisons there was. It had ranked in the top five of the nation's most brutal prisons. It was reserved for hard heads and big timers! I asked to see my counselor, but that was laughed off and within an hour I was on the BlueBird headed for one of the deadliest prisons in America. When you look at the old jail from the outside, it looks like a castle set in old England. Some cons took to calling it Castle Grayskull. It was an intimidating-looking place to say the least, and I was more than a little concerned. I was in for a cold reception anyway because my brother already had a reputation for being a hardhead, so as soon as they saw my name the guards took an instant dislike to me.

I climbed off the bus, my chains clanking as I shuffled through the front door of the ugly building with two other prisoners following me. "Line up single file!" the big redneck in a prison guard uniform and leather vest barked at us. We lined up best we could considering we were tethered side by side by chains.

"Hey, city boy, do you know what single file means?" another guard said putting his nose inches from mine.

Before I could answer I was shoved through a doorway and up against the wall. The guards slammed the door shut and walked away, leaving us in the small room still chained six ways from Sunday. About thirty minutes later they came back in, the big cop sucking his teeth and chewing a toothpick. I guess we interrupted his lunch. As they removed the chains, they pushed and pulled me around, yelling commands the whole time. I was so tired I barely cared about the treatment; I just wanted the steel off me and a place to lie down.

A black dude came in the room. He had on street clothes, and I wasn't sure if he was a guard or not, but he started asking us questions and filling out papers. When he asked me a question, I answered with a quiet "Yes, sir."

The room went quiet and I could feel eyes on me as I looked up to see what had happened. Then I felt the huge hand of the leather vest guard wrap around my throat. He slammed me back against the wall. "The only people you call sir wear a blue uniform." He screamed at me, spittle flying in my face. I was caught off-guard. I mean, I never imagined I'd get in trouble for speaking to someone with respect.

I nodded the best I could with his big hand wrapped around my throat and croaked out a "Yes, sir." A smile of satisfaction spread across his face as he let go and finished unhooking me. The black guy looked at me apologetically and continued his questions that I answered with yes and no. The guards left the room while he gave us two flat sheets, a wool blanket, a roll of toilet paper and assigned us a cell location. He said, "Man, you can't call a nigga sir around here." He laughed as he said it, but he knew I wasn't a racist, and he gave me a bottom bunk on F-2, a tier on the south side of the prison. His name was Cleveland, and we would go on to become good friends. He had gotten used to the racist guards and kept his mouth shut so he had a job as a shotcaller, assigning bunks and such. It was a good job because if someone wanted to move, they had to see Cleveland, and depending on the location or whose cell it was, the price could go as high as fifty bucks or three cartons of cigarettes. Prison politics; more on that later

As I walked to my tier, carrying my bedroll with me, I looked around and will say this: it was clean! The floors were buffed to a nice shine; even the bars were polished brass on the thruway grills. There was a grill every few feet, and a different guard on each tier had to unlock it with a huge, old-time key. Each guard's mood dictated how long it took you to move through the prison. As I got to my tier and really got a chance to see the little cells, panic set in! I couldn't believe that I was going to spend five years in one of these little rooms. It wasn't like the movies with steel bars and all that. It does look like that at the penitentiary, but here they had solid steel doors with a small window and two crossbars in the windows! They told me my cell was the last one on the right-hand side. I walked toward it with my heart pumping, and as I neared the cell, the guard pulled a lever from inside a lockbox at the top of the tier. The doors weren't electric, so when the guard pulled the lever, it just popped open, but you had to open and close your own cell. I tell you this because I never did get used to locking myself in.

In my cell was a white dude who was balding on top but had super long hair in the back. His name was Tommy. We made small talk while I made my bed. He was friendly, which I didn't expect. I wouldn't get my TV, cigarettes, clothes and all personal property till the next day. The lady who searched everything and gave you your stuff back wouldn't be in till then, so I asked Tommy if he had a cigarette. He threw me his can of tobacco, and I rolled myself a smoke. He gave me a bar of soap, and I washed my hands and face. I felt much better after I cleaned up and had a cigarette. Tommy even offered me a cup of coffee, but I didn't feel like going though the process of heating up the water, which I will explain in a little while. I told Tommy I'd pay him back the next day when they returned my property, and he said that was cool. He said roll a cigarette anytime I wanted; after all a big can of tobacco only cost two dollars back then. I was feeling much better when I lay back on my bunk. Tommy was standing by the sink. He looked straight at me and said, "I bet a nice blowjob would put you right to sleep. Can I hook you up?"

## Chapter 15
## Dirty Deeds

I jumped to my feet and threw my hands up to fight. I saw the fear register in his eyes. "I'm sorry, man, I just thought..."

He wouldn't finish the sentence. I had him pinned to the door with my forearm across his throat. With my other hand I grabbed his hair and said, "Listen, bitch, I don't play that faggot shit. If you ever try any gay shit with me, I'll kill you in this motherfuckin' cell!!" He apologized and promised never to say anything to me again. I let him go, but drove my point home with a nice slap to the face.

"You don't have to hit me" he squealed.

"I need you to understand just how serious I am" I said, pushing away from him.

"I get it, I get it!" he said as I glared at him. This was definitely not minimum security anymore. There was lots of homosexual behavior, lots of violence and some jerk always wanting to see what the new guy was made of. The question wasn't, "Is he a great fighter?", it's "Will he stand up for himself?"

They wouldn't have long to wait for those answers from me.

The next day, I went down to get my property, I had

accumulated quite a bit of stuff at Patuxent because when you get transferred, your money takes a couple weeks to catch up to you. I loaded my things in a big laundry basket on wheels. Setting my TV on top—the best TV in the jail because my mother had a Zenith 19" color TV, but the old jail only sold 13 inch and most of the time they had black and white. You had to get on a waiting list to get a color TV. As I wheeled onto the tier, everyone was locked in waiting for count to finish so they could go back to the rec hall or their job. They count all the time and on every shift. After a few years, it seems like prison is just one super-long count!

As I made my way down the tier pushing my cart, there was a dark-skinned guy standing at his door. As I passed by he said, "Hey, you can move in my cell anytime." After the deal with my cellmate the night before, I was starting to believe the jail was loaded with homosexuals.

He stood there smiling at me, so I said, "We can talk about it when the doors hit," hoping to scare him a little bit.

He just smiled and said, "That's a bet."

As I walked away, I was perplexed. This guy didn't seem the least bit worried about our "talk," and as I got to my cell, I kept turning it over in my head, getting angrier with each passing moment. Now I never was a great fighter, but I knew in this place I had to stand up for myself. I was getting more psyched up for the coming fight. I pictured me running in his cell and hitting him with a solid overhand right; his knees would buckle, and then I'd teach him not to mess with me.

Things rarely go as planned, and this was to be no exception. The doors opened. I pulled mine open and quickly headed for the dude's cell. I passed by Cleveland, the guy who gave me my cell assignment. I quickly made a mental note to see him about the guy he put me in the cell with. The dark-skinned guy was about to step out of his cell when I stepped to him and fired a stiff right hand straight at his jaw, hoping to knock him out or at least stun the hell out of him. He was fast, very fast and moved to where I got a glancing blow to the side of his face. He pulled me in the cell and the fight was on! It was a flurry of fists thrown, more of them coming from him then me as we grappled in the confined space. I knew I was on the verge of a serious beat down when a body came in between us. "That's enough, guys. Neither one of you wanna go to lockup."

I was happy that someone broke it up, but I had to stay tough. I backed out of the cell, telling the guy he was lucky someone broke it up, and him telling me the same. As I looked at the dude who broke up the fight, I noticed for the first time it was Cleveland.

"Get to your cell and clean up. I'll get the C.O. to open the door in like twenty minutes so that you can come to the rec hall." I passed by the onlookers holding my head up. I didn't care that I was a little beat up. What mattered was I was willing to fight if I felt disrespected. The weak were preyed upon, and I wasn't for it. I cleaned up once I got to my cell and got a look at my face. Aside from a busted lip and a little swelling, I didn't look too bad. I lit a cigarette and set down. I didn't know what would happen when I went to the rec hall. Would the dark-skinned guy want to fight? Would he want to shank me when I wasn't looking? I was about to find out.

The door hit and I grabbed my cup. I threw a spoon of instant coffee and two sugar cubes in it and headed for the rec hall. They had a big coffee pot in a steal cage with strategically cut areas allowing you to get hot water for your coffee or oodles of noodles, but so you couldn't pick it up and throw the hot water on someone. Cleveland approached me as I came in the rec hall. "Listen, the dude you hit is a cool brother. We call him Black, and he just wants to know if it's over. He says he don't know why you hit him."

I looked at Cleveland trying to read him, looking for signs of insincerity, but I saw nothing but genuine concern, which shocked me. "I don't play them homosexual games. I'm not a fag and anyone who approaches me with that gay shit, I'm gonna fight, and I don't care if I win, lose or draw!" I said with a look I hoped conveyed how serious I was.

Cleveland said, "I think you got something twisted. Black don't play that gay shit. Let's go talk to him and get this straight." I was nervous walking over toward him. He was sitting at a table by himself with a drawing book and a bunch of colored pencils. I spoke first, my voice almost cracking from fear, but I held it together while I fired my words out in rapid succession. "Look, man, I'm not gay and when you said I could move in your cell, I thought you were looking for a punk."

He just smiled a huge smile and said, "Dude, you read that all wrong, I didn't say you could move in my cell 'cause of any gay shit. You got the biggest TV in the jail. I seen it sitting on top of your property. I'm in a cell without a TV. It makes for a long day"

I laughed a bit more nervously than I liked, but they quickly fell in with laughter of their own. Before long we were all laughing at my silliness. Black and I spent the next few years telling each other how lucky the other was that Cleveland broke up the fight that morning. That is to say we went on to be friends, and down the road I would be grateful to have him as a friend!

Cleveland and I became friends, as well. He liked that I didn't see color. Here's the thing about prison—it is a place made up of different "cliques" and everybody stays with their own. You got the white guys, and they are usually the bikers, the Aryans and nowadays gangs such as D.M.I. or Dead Man Incorporated (that was actually started by a childhood friend of mine). The black guys become Muslims or B.G.F., which is Black Guerilla Family, as well as Crips and Bloods. When I was doing my time, we didn't have the gangs in Maryland like they do today, but it definitely had its cliques. The bikers and the Muslims were always present, and the separation of black and white people was a great divide! I cruised along, staying to myself and under the radar for about thirty days, but then I made a decision that could have ended my young life!

## Chapter 16
## Long Road Home

    I was young and really hung up on not being disrespected. I would find myself in a situation where I could have just acted like I didn't notice the blatant disrespect and walked away, but that wasn't me. I wasn't going to let it slide, because if you let it go once, people become bolder and will try to prey on that weakness. I was at the old jail for about a month, maybe six weeks, and I was starting to get into a little pattern, I would come out at first rec hall and take my shower just before lock in, then I'd get dressed and such while they took count and, then I'd go to second rec hall and not have to worry about rushing to get a shower before lockdown.
    As I headed to the six-man shower, I noticed there was one other guy in, there but that wasn't unusual, I just had never paid this dude much attention. He was about 6' 3" and a good 260 lbs. and no fat on him at all. He had a matching nickname like "Freight Train" or "Dump Truck" that I can't quite remember, but anyway I went about taking my shower when I caught movement out of the corner of my eye. Always aware of my surroundings, I knew the movement looked out of place, but now it's decision time. Do I act like I don't see it or do I confront it

head on? I looked at the big black man as he stood maybe ten feet from me masturbating furiously. I was shocked, but held my composure. "Hey, man, you gotta stop that while I'm in here," I said in an even tone more shocked than afraid.

He said, "This ain't got nothin' to do with you, white boy!"

He then turned his back to me and kept jerking off. I was furious, but this was a big dude and he was showing me that not only would he disrespect me, but that he had no fear of me by turning his back on me.

In the corner of the shower was a bucket with a detachable ringer to remove excess water from the mop. The sanitation guy filled his bucket up in the shower and cleaned it afterward, so it stayed in the shower when not in use. I grabbed the heavy ringer trying not to make any noise and headed toward a man that got bigger with each step. Fear flooded through me 'cause if this dude turns around, he would undoubtedly beat me up, and given the circumstances, it could get really ugly from there. He sensed my movement a fraction of a second too late. I swung the mop ringer with a two-handed full swing aimed at his lower back. It hit with a solid impact, and he went straight to the ground, the wind leaving his body in a half scream, half gasp sort of sound. I pulled back and swung a second time. He had no defense as the heavy metal ringer crashed across his upper back and shoulders. I pulled back for my next swing. It would be the coup de grace 'cause I was aiming for his head. I was in mid-swing when the guard tackled me and took me to the ground. "It's over Fred. You won, you won." I heard his words for the first time as I allowed myself to be cuffed. My opponent was sprawled out on the floor unable to move, let alone get up.

They led me through three rec halls completely naked and down to the area called "the back keys." As they dragged me through the recreation areas I got whistles and cat calls and more than a few laughs, but the laughing stopped when they wheeled my opponent through on a stretcher. He was moaning and sobbing. I never knew how much damage a mop ringer could do until that day! They took me to the back keys and threw me in a cell. A guard grabbed me some clothes from the laundry room and I was grateful to have them. When you get in a fight or get in trouble in jail, you're given what's known as a "ticket"—a written report of your rule infraction. In a few days you go to the "adjustment board" and depending on the category of your offense, an independent hearing officer gives you your punishment, which can be anything from a verbal warning to loss of good time and time in solitary confinement! At the time a fight ticket was 30/30: you lose thirty days good time and you get thirty days in solitary, also known as "lockup" or "the hammer."

We both received the same sentence. During our hearing he admitted to masturbating in the shower, but argued that since he never threw a punch, he shouldn't get lockup time. The hearing officer disagreed, but wrote everything down, giving us copies. That would save my life in a few short weeks. As I finished my lockup time, a guy brought me a note from Cleveland. He said he would bring me back to my old cell, but that I had a big problem. The guy I hit with a mop ringer was a Muslim! You have to understand prison politics to see the danger, which I didn't understand at that time. This particular group of Muslims believed that the white man was the devil. It's a sect built on hating white people. They spend their time blaming the white man for everything, and the fact that I, a white man, had hurt a Muslim put me on the hit list. I was to be stabbed my first day in gen pop!

It seems everyone knew this, including the guards. I was the only one blind to the fact. Thank God Cleveland put me wise to it. The day I came off lockup I felt like a leper. No one would get within six feet of me; they just knew I was dead as soon as I hit that yard. That afternoon before yard time, Cleveland and Black, the only friends I had at the moment, were taping hard-back book covers to my chest, intended to protect my vital organs in the inevitable knife fight. Prepping me for the yard, the guards would pat me down, but they would be looking for steel, so the books would be fine under a hoodie. After the search I was to find Black in the yard to get the ice pick from him, and then it would be time to go straight at them!

Just before the doors hit for evening yard, Cleveland said, "Listen, Fred, you don't have to do this. There's a lot of serious dudes on protective custody because they didn't want to mess with the Muslims." I knew he was telling the truth as he continued, "Just go to the tier guard and tell him you want to go on p.c. Hell, they already know why."

I shook my head. I just couldn't live like that. I still had four years left, and I wasn't about to do it on the chicken farm, as it was often called. When the doors opened, my heart jumped and my stomach felt hollow as I made my way to the front grill. My mind was racing, and I have to say that the whole protective custody idea was sounding much better. But I knew I couldn't go out like that. A coward dies a million deaths, but when you're standing there and your ticket is about to really be punched, fear starts talking louder and louder! As I started through the door and into the yard, two guards pulled me out of line to pat me down. "Frederick, it appears you've gained weight." They chuckled at how clever they were as hands passed over the hard-back books.

Then one of them pushed me toward the yard. I was scanning the crowd looking for Black. I didn't see him anywhere! Panic set in. I needed that shank or I was a dead man. Hell, I was probably dead anyway, but at least with the knife I had a chance to strike back. Then I caught sight of him. He was moving toward me and everyone else was moving away. As we passed, he handed me the homemade knife, which I quickly slipped into my hoodie pocket. As I walked the yard, I took notice of how far the bikers and other white factions stayed from me. I noticed the guards all stood looking in my direction, and yes, I was afraid, but I was angry that everyone just wanted to see the show and absolutely no one—with the exception of Black and Cleveland—cared one bit what happened to me. Cleveland walked over to me. Our eyes met and I said, "Look, brother, you've done more for me than anyone, but this I gotta do on my own."

Before he could answer, a guy the color of midnight walked up to us, and looking me in the eye said, "Pye wants to see you over by the monkey bars."

I looked straight back into his eyes, refusing to show fear. I said my first racist thing ever: "How appropriate." That was it, the time had come—when Pye called you over, very few returned.

Chapter 17
Don't Damn Me

So many things ran through my mind as I headed toward the monkey bars, but mostly fear was at the forefront of my mind. I know there's people who would claim they weren't afraid, but for me, my insides were shaking and my nerves were on high alert. I have never been so aware in my life. All there was at that moment was the moment—it was the truest form of living in the now I've ever experienced. As I walked up to Pye, I noticed how big he was. I had seen him around the jail, and I knew he was the leader of the Muslims, but standing there with his shirt off, his muscles bulging from just finishing a set of pull-ups, he looked huge. Pye was one of the most powerful guys in the prison system. He could get someone killed in any institution with the nod of his head. He had been in prison since he was sixteen years old, and his release date was set for never! He was doing multiple life sentences, and he didn't smoke, curse or partake in homosexual activity. In the big scheme of things, I was not a blip on his radar. I wasn't plugged in with any group and my death wouldn't put him in anyone's bad grace.

As I approached him, I wasn't sure if I would get a chance to say anything or how this would go down. A big smile broke out on his face when he saw me approaching. "You are either the dumbest devil I've ever seen or the bravest. Do you know who I am?"

I nodded and said, "I know who you are, and I'm starting to think I'm the dumbest."

His smile broadened and he said, "Why didn't you go on the Duece?" That's prison slang for protective custody.

"Just ain't me." I croaked out, and the smile left his face instantly. He started toward me and my fight or flee reflexes started battling one another. Just as I was about to pull my knife out he stopped.

"You hit a Muslim. You put your filthy devil hands on one of my beautiful black brothers!" "Yes, I did, but I didn't know he was with you, and he was jerking off, so I'd do it again."  He leered at me. "What did you say?" His gaze burned through me as fear shot to my rolling stomach.

I looked him in the eye and said, "Any man jerking off while I'm in the shower will get exactly what he got." My voice held steady, but my insides were quaking.

Pye looked over his shoulder and told his lieutenant to get the guy I hit. He walked over all smiles, but his smile faded fast when Pye said, "Were you masturbating while this man was in the shower?"

What I didn't know is the Muslims really frown on that sorta thing. A Muslim can be kicked out for this behavior; it's a super big no-no! The guy looked at his feet and mumbled something, but Pye wasn't letting it go. At that moment, my very life hung in the balance. "Were you masturbating in the shower when this man struck you, I want the whole story now."

I interrupted and said, "Listen, I didn't hit a guy with a mop ringer for no reason. I told him to stop. He turned his back on me and kept going, so I did what I had to, and I have a copy of my ticket where he admits to it."

Pye glared at his fellow Muslim. "Your silence says

much."

Finally the man responded, "I was, Pye. The European is telling the truth." European is a nice way of saying white boy amongst the Muslim sect.

Pye's next words were like getting a pardon from the governor. "You're free to go your way, but if you ever have a problem with another Muslim, you see me first."

I agreed and extended my hand. He looked at my hand for a full thirty seconds before reaching out and shaking it. His giant hand enveloped mine and a respect was forged that would save me again a little down the road.

As I walked away, the yard was full of electricity. The guards in the towers put their guns back on safety and every eye was on me. Cleveland and Black were the first to approach, throwing their arms around me. I never would have believed that I could make true friends in prison, but here they were slapping me on the back and laughing with me. Cleveland said, "Well, son, the bikers and every other peckerwood (white guys) crew is gonna want you on their team. You beat up a Mo brotha and lived to tell about it. You just became a big dog."

Sure enough, by the time the yard ended I had three white dudes approach me to ask for a "sit down" (a formal talk) as soon as possible. I had a real problem with this and voiced my disdain to Cleveland. "Those guys wouldn't come near me when they thought I was a dead man walking. Not one of them offered advice or a piece of steel. I'm not joining up with some half-ass biker clique."

Cleveland listened and said, "You may want to think about that. You could negotiate your way into a second in command position, and then you get a piece of the dope action, the gambling and the protection rackets. IT could be a profitable proposition for you."

I knew he was right, but I had my own dope connection. My mom was bringing a bundle a week, and I didn't have to split it with anyone. I just had to keep it quiet 'cause jealous dudes love to snitch. I weighed the pros and cons of joining some clique and decided I was best suited to do my own thing. No one was gonna tell me I couldn't associate with Black or Cleveland. Those guys were my friends when no one wanted to be! Yes, there were bonuses to hooking up with a crew, but it just wasn't my style, and I got a lot of respect for it. When the black dudes heard I wouldn't run with a racist clique, they liked me, and the whites respected my strength, meaning we could still do business together from time to time. I fell into a rhythm after my first two months and things were going well. A little too well.

Some people found out about my mom bringing heroin to the jail after seeing me stoned out of my mind on visiting day a few weeks running. It wasn't difficult to put things together. I agreed to sell some, but I just couldn't meet demand and someone always got left out. It would start on Thursday, two days before my visit. Guys would line up with cartons of cigarettes trying to get in first. Before long, someone snitched and things went bad. My mom came up on a Saturday, and they were waiting on her. They searched her six ways from Sunday coming in, but didn't find the ten balloons of high-grade heroin in her bra. They let her in to visit me and were watching every move, but I got the balloons and swallowed them. She was scheduled to come back that afternoon. I went back to my cell and as luck would have it, I couldn't throw up the balloons, so I just had to wait on nature. But this was no big deal. I'd just get the dope the next day.

They called me for my afternoon visit, and I was glad that the dope part was over. As I walked up the stairs, I saw six guards and a dog at the top in front of the visiting room. They pulled me in a room and stripped me down and looked me over from top to bottom. Then the one guard informed me I didn't have a visit, but that my mother had been locked up outside the jail. I would later find out that while she was in visiting me the dog had alerted on her pocketbook stored in a locker where the visitors check in. There was a small amount of dope she held back for the girl that drove her up to see me, which was the same girl going to see my brother and who had introduced my mother to skin popping . My heart sank as I thought about my mom being placed in cuffs. I called in a few favors and got a telephone call around 10:00 p.m. that night. It was difficult to get on the phone back then, but I was ecstatic when I heard my mom pick up the phone and accept my collect call. "Mom, are you OK?"

I stammered, but my mom being the true outlaw she was, uttered two words that started me laughing hysterically. "Fuck 'em."

## Chapter 18
## Years Go By

My mom was a lot of things, and by society's standards, she was a terrible mother, but I never doubted her love for me. I always knew Steve was the apple of her eye, but I knew my mom loved me. When I was a kid, I would sit in so many hospital waiting rooms praying to God, asking Him not to take her away. I wasn't a dumb kid. I had heard the double talk around the house, about my mom being a former prostitute on the notorious "block." I must admit that those stories shaped my view of women for many years. My mom was not on the PTA or any other boards; she was "The Greek's" wife, a title that got her first-class service in some circles, but shunned in others. Whatever your view of my mother, I want to make it clear I never doubted that my mom would have done my sentence for me if she could. She was limited in many areas. She wasn't refined or elegant. She was a Budweiser girl with champagne taste, but when she had an opportunity for champagne, she wouldn't know what kind to order.

Her murder trial would come up while I was in prison (http://articles.baltimoresun.com/1992-02-25/news/1992056021_1_lacey-double-jeopardy-mrs). She would choose to go in front of a judge this time and let him decide the case instead of a jury trial. After both sides presented their case, the judge ruled in my mother's favor. He blasted the prosecution's Cliff Robertson, saying there was absolutely no evidence connecting my mother to my father's murder. John had already pled guilty and received a thirty-year sentence. When they brought him into my mother's trial, he refused to answer any questions, which speaks to his character. He could have said he acted alone, but he wouldn't say anything. What a dirty little man he is. My mother was the only person on the planet who held a single shred of love for him, and he wouldn't testify to clear her. My mother walked out a free woman; whether she was truly innocent I'll never know. She took the details to her grave, and if John Lacey ever did decide to talk about it, who could believe a word out of his mouth? Anyway, she returned to my father's house flush with the cash the insurance company now had to pay because of the acquittal.

All her boys were in prison, and since she wasn't allowed to visit me anymore, and John was way up in Cumberland, Maryland, she went to see Stevie a few times a week—her and Steve's junkie girl that Steve thought was a princess. Mom would take him dope and money, but he would later say no one ever came to see him. His version of the truth has nothing to do with reality, but that guy could do no wrong in my mother's eyes.

I was maybe six or nine months into my sentence, and things were progressing along— until my run-in with a redneck guard named Johnson, who turned my life into a living hell! He was one of the guards on the shakedown crew, and I was pretty much off their list since my mom was busted, but I still had dope coming into the jail. I had a buddy of mine get his girl to stop by my mother's house twice a month to pick up a package of heroin and pills. She would smuggle them in to the inmate who took photos in the visiting room. Neither of them got high, so it was an under-the-radar operation, and I was turning a nice profit and cruising along. Then my luck took take a turn for the worse. It started over a cup of water, of all things.

In the chow hall, they had a version of Kool-Aid that tasted like medicine, so I never drank the stuff. I would take my cup and after everyone sat down, I would walk up to get my water. Well, on this day, the guard Johnson was running the chow lines. When I headed to get my water, Johnson yelled, "Sit down, convict!"

I didn't think he was talking to meat first, but as soon as I realized it was me he was talking to I said, "Johnson, I'm just getting a cup of water, relax."

He looked at me like I was a piece of trash and said, "Gimme your ID."

All prisoners are required to have their prison identification card on them at all times, but I just happened to leave mine in my cell that day. "I don't have it. Are you writing me up over a glass of water? What the fuck is wrong with you, Johnson?" I went back to my table, shaking my head.

After chow lines ran, I was in my cell getting ready to go to the small yard when Johnson appeared at my door. "Where's your ID?" I smiled at the silliness of it all and handed him my ID.

As he walked off the tier, someone yelled, "Get off the tier, you flat-footed bitch!"

"You got another ticket for disrespect. Do you wanna try for three?" Johnson said to me.

"Man, you know that wasn't me!" I protested, but he walked off the tier to write me a three-page ticket.

I was sitting in my cell seething when the door opened and Johnson handed me the ticket. "Sign it," he demanded. I grabbed the ticket and tore it up. I don't recall who swung first, but soon we were fighting man to man, and I was whipping his ass in that small cell. In the struggle, he keyed his radio and sent out an officer-in-distress code. In seconds, I heard the "goon squad" headed for my cell. I threw my final punch right to the nose of the correctional officer, a punch I would regret for quite some time.

The "goon squad" is a name given to the tactical response team by the prisoners. They only come for fights or stabbings, and when they show up, the convicts are getting the beating of a lifetime. When they seen Johnson coming flying out of my cell from my last punch, his face a bloody mess, tears streaming involuntarily from the shot to the nose, they took it very personally. They beat on me for like fifteen minutes. By the time they were done, I had a broken nose, two split lips and a few broken ribs. Swelling had already set in, and I looked like a car accident victim. They were out of breath as they cuffed me and dragged me to lockup, smacking me and kicking me along the way. As I got to the lockup cell, they pulled the door open and uncuffed me. I turned in time to see a baton headed at my head, a flash of white light went off and everything went black.

As I came to, a black fog lifted and pain like you would not believe set in, I couldn't pinpoint my pain because my entire body was racked with agony. I slowly got up off the cement floor, each move causing me to cry out. The room started to spin as I got to my feet. I had to sit on the bunk and gather myself before I slipped into unconsciousness. After a few moments, I reached the sink and started to wash the dried blood from my face. I had no idea how long I lay on the floor knocked out by the guards, but when I heard the grill at the top of the tier open and the shuffle of the goon squads' boots, I figured they were bringing someone else to lockup, and I said a little prayer that they weren't coming for me.

My prayer would go unanswered.

## Chapter 19
## Thunderstruck

    I cannot describe the pain inflicted on me. It's very hard to believe that a person can be beaten the way I was and not only survive, but stay conscious for most of it. When my door opened and the realization that the goon squad was back for a second round of unmerciful beating, a little urine escaped my bladder, I haven't felt such dread since my childhood when my father summoned me to him for a "talk." The "tac team" spent no time with preliminaries. They came straight in, beating on me, flashes of light exploding in my head as blows rained down on me. It was like jolts of lighting flashing across my nerves while thunder exploded in my head. I really couldn't see much—my eyes were swelled to slits, the beating went on for a lifetime and, as they tired of beating on me, I welcomed the blackness that threatened to consume me. I wasn't sure if I was dying or passing out, but I desperately wanted the punches and kicks to stop. Soon, I felt the blows stop, and I heard their boots retreating. I heard one say, "Is he dead?" Another summed up the feeling of the entire group of sadists: "Fuck him."

    I lay there, drifting in and out of consciousness. I have no idea how much time passed; there were fleeting moments of extreme pain only to drift back into the blissful darkness. I felt myself being lifted. I knew I was alive because of the pain, and for some reason, I thought it was the early hours of morning because as we rolled through the open grills, I saw no one in the rec halls as I forced my eyes to open. "Stay with us, Freddie." I heard a kind voice say and tears streamed down my face. Another voice said, "He's crying," and then the gentle voice again, "You would be, too."

As they wheeled me into a brightly lit room, I cried out as the light sent shock waves of pain into my eyes. "Load him up with Demerol," the kind voice shouted.

"But we don't know how much trauma his head sustained," the second voice said.

"Look, he may not make it anyway. Let's get him comfortable."

Those words terrified me, but they brought out my fighters spirit. I vowed to myself that I wouldn't die in that prison, not on this day anyway! I felt a flood of warm relief spread through my body, the narcotic easing every screaming nerve. It didn't stop the pain, but it made the pain bearable. I have no idea what was done to save my life; there's no official record of me being in the prison hospital for three weeks. The story that went out was that I had not paid a drug debt and was found in my cell beaten nearly to death, and that I owed my life to the immediate response of the tac team that saved me and delivered me to the infirmary for the best possible care. Let me tell you this—there are a lot of guys who got killed in that prison by the guards, and their families were told similar fairy tales. As for my case, a respected officer of twenty-four years signed the one official incident report and that would never be questioned.

When I was finally released back to general population, I was given a hero's welcome. Everyone knew what happened, and it was a well-known fact that people had disappeared under similar circumstances. I was still pretty swelled up, and they gave me a big pair of sunglasses to help with the light sensitivity. Between the glasses and a cane I had to use for a few months, I looked like a blind man. Cleveland and Black were constantly at my side, and everyone was looking out for me, going to get my coffee and carrying my commissary for me, I walked into the chow hall with my cane and big glasses when a lieutenant they called Jimmy Dean, a real by-the-book correctional officer approached and said, "What are doing wearing sunglasses indoors?"

I smiled, wondering why he had just noticed. "Sorry, sir, I'm covering my raccoon eyes."

I removed the glasses, revealing my swollen and still discolored eyes. "My God, son, what happened to you?"

I really thought he was being an asshole and I spat my words out without thinking, "Ask your tac team!" I spat the words.

"Are you saying my officers did this?" With his question hanging in the air, he turned his back and walked away.

I ate my lunch and went back to my cell. I was still on medication and soon the nurse would be by to give me my afternoon dose. I would then probably lay down till dinner time. The nurse opened my door, and we exchanged pleasantries as she gave me my meds. The guard at the top of the tier yelled to me, "After you take your meds, they want you down back keys."

As I ambled toward back keys, I wondered what they wanted with me. I also noticed the guards giving me dirty looks, but I wasn't sure why. I passed by the last grill before back keys, where a little, fat guard said, "Hey, Fred, five years can turn into a long bit without friends,"

I didn't understand what he meant, but my wit never

wavered. "I didn't know I had any in the first place."

As I got to back keys, I was directed to an office with Lieutenant Jimmy Dean and, of all people, Officer Johnson. "I want to know what happened to you," the lieutenant said in his matter-of-fact tone. I thought I had stepped into The Twilight Zone, and I just stood there staring at him. "If my officers did this, you have my word they will be held accountable. Just give me their names and sign this complaint. I promise you there will be no reprisals!"

I honestly thought he was joking, but after a full minute of silence, I could see he was sincere. I looked him straight in the eye and said, "I'd like to go lay down." He glared at me, and I sat there impassively as he started talking about right and wrong and how officers should set an example. After he finished, I said "Sir, I just took my medicine. Can I please go lay down?"

"I know you're scared, Freddie." Yes, he called me Freddie, and for some reason it infuriated me.

"Look, I'm not your fuckin' kid, I'm not your fuckin' snitch, and only my friends call me Freddie, I told you that I'm not going to sign a complaint, and I meant it. Now may I please return to my cell?" I didn't wait for an answer as I got up and headed for the door.

"Inmate 197746 returning to his cell!" the lieutenant yelled, and a guard opened the door. As I made my way back, I neither felt good or bad about the exchange between me and Jimmy Dean. It was just a misplaced sense of logic; never snitch on anyone, even if it's guards and you're the victim. The correctional officers were under a microscope at the time for beating a dude nearly to death over at the new jail. They punctured his lung, and when it started filling with blood, one of the guards called an ambulance. At the hospital, the convict told internal affairs the entire story, and in that piss-ant town, that was front page news. Unfortunately, the convict was killed in a prison uprising a few months later, with all charges against officers dismissed due to lack of evidence. That was Hagerstown in the '80s; I really hope the guys are treated better these days.

I had no idea the impact of my meeting with the lieutenant, but as always, I was soon to find out. The first sign of things to come was the little fat cop who had told me how long five years can be was standing there smiling with the grill open for me to pass. There was a sanitation guy buffing the floors; the fat guard said, "Hey, inmate, get out of Fred's way! Can't you see him trying to pass?" I looked at him wondering what had him in such a good mood. I had no idea word had already spread that I didn't snitch, and suddenly, from a month or so before, when I was the most hated man in the jail, I was suddenly a stand-up guy in the eyes of the blacks, the whites and even the guards. Man, life is crazy!!!

Chapter 20
Happy Trails

My time started zipping by. I knew they wouldn't give me parole, so I had to get as much good time as possible. I went to school during the day, and in the evening, split my time between the music room and the weightlifting team. School paid 1.10 per day, but you got ten days a month good time. After the first semester , my teachers felt like I was ready to take my GED test, but I pulled them to the side and asked them to let me stay in class to get the good days, and they agreed. The chip on my shoulder was gone for the moment and most people liked me. Even the gangs I refused to join respected me for riding alone. I took up reading, and my teacher brought me all the classics, *Moby Dick, A Tale of Two Cities,* the Anne Frank diary and many more. I tore through them. I loved *The Adventures of Huckleberry Finn.* It transported me out of that dank, ugly prison, and suddenly I was going down the river with Huckleberry Finn. I was in the attic with a scared little girl coming of age, or I was on my own island creating a democracy. Books were an escape for me, and I became quite the reader. IT was coupled by my thirst for knowledge about all things like politics and secret societies, the Illuminati and the Masons. My teachers fed my interest and couldn't understand what a nice boy like me was doing in prison.

The truth is, I thrived in prison at that time. I was staying away from drugs and getting in great shape. My mind was expanding, and I was looking at the world through new eyes. Before long, my transfer to minimum security came through. I looked back at three years that seemingly flew by. I went to a place called Jessup Pre-Release Unit or J.P.R.U., as it's more often called. It was five buildings with two big dorms on each side of the buildings, with the exception of the one building that was the chow hall/visiting room. The officers were in the main building, as well. Around back were the commissary and multi-purpose rooms where they held school, church and gave out packages. They had a nice little weightlifting area, a full-court basketball court and a little area for playing volleyball where most of the white guys hung out. Convicts jokingly referred to it as "Cracker Beach." The jail itself was a world away from MCI-H. You could carry cash on you and go to the commissary anytime the yard was open. You were allowed four visits a week, and your family could bring six-canned items and food from outside that had to be eaten on the visit. Compared to where I came, from it felt like a Hilton hotel.

I got in school again for the good time, and the teacher, seeing some potential, had me take the high-school test instead of the GED, and she was very happy with the results. I was the highest-scoring person out of all the jails in Jessup, which was a feather in her cap. I got a real diploma instead of the GED equivalency, which I was very proud of. I still had two years left, and my luck would take a turn for the worse, but didn't it always?

J.P.R.U. had pay phones. You could drop a quarter in and call home. So one day I was bored and called a friend named Brenda. She answered the phone, and I could tell something was wrong. When I pressed her, she said someone was there and wanted to speak to me. Next thing I know, I hear the voice of my codefendant from the script-busting charge. The last time I saw him was at the county jail where he was terrified. I asked the cop to put us on the same section 'cause he was about to burst into tears. The cop complied, and I babysat him till his mother paid his bail. He repaid me by signing a statement against me saying the script and everything was mine. He got a suspended sentence, and I went to prison.

To say I was shocked when I heard his voice is a huge understatement. He started telling me how good he was doing and how sorry he was for snitching on me. I sat there listening. I had planned my revenge for the past three-and-a-half years and now this dude was right on the phone saying he wanted to come visit me. I scheduled his visit for the end of the week, I told him to bring me ten balloons of heroin and sixty dollars. I also wanted a pizza from Squires with everything except anchovies. He agreed to my request and got right to work on getting me the dope. I had a girl coming to see me midweek, where I told her that I had a ticket and would be going to lockup for thirty days, so I would write her and then give her a call when they put me back in population.

The day of the visit I packed all my stuff up and went around saying my goodbyes to the friends I had made while being there. Some tried to talk me out of it, but most understood my logic. I've lived by this motto: if you don't stand for something, you'll fall for anything. Plus, I was young and caught up in the 'snitches get stitches' mentality. Like most people in jail, I blamed everyone else for my incarceration. It was only after my journey into the 12 Steps that I took ownership of my shit. That would be a few years off and at that moment, I wanted blood. As I walked into the visiting room, I noticed how out of shape he was.

His arms looked like spaghetti strands. He smiled widely and was headed in to hug me when I shot my hand out to shake hands. I didn't want this mutt to wrap those skinny arms around me. I sat down and he handed me cash; I put it in my pocket. He then started handing me balloons. I always had trouble swallowing those damn balloons! If it were a piece of steak, it wouldn't have been a problem, but just knowing it's a foreign object made it very difficult. He was telling me how two grams of raw dope cost him nearly five hundred dollars. As I got the last one down, I nearly lost it and threw them up, which would have been really bad for many reasons , I managed to get them down and listened as he babbled on about how happy he was we were still friends.

I took a bite of my pizza, but knowing what I was about to do had made eating difficult. I hadn't said ten words since sitting down, but he liked to talk and rambled right along. He had begun to tell me about this 18-year-old girl he was banging and said he would send me some naked pictures if I wanted. Fury rose in me as I thought about him out there having sex and partying. It wasn't fair at all. *He* brought me the script, *he* didn't tell me they had tried to fill it before, *he* wrote the damn thing, and here *I* was rotting in jail, missing my early 20s while this coward was out there living like Hugh Hefner!

He was in total shock when I threw a massive overhand right straight to his unprotected nose. Blood gushed as he fell off the chair to the floor. I was on him immediately with a flurry of lefts and rights, and I heard the police rushing in my direction. I went for the coup de grace—I threw a right hand that would make Holyfield proud, using my lat and shoulder to deliver as much force to his already battered face as I could. The hit sounded with a thud. I wanted to break his jaw, to hurt what he used against me, but had to settle for shredded lips and a broken nose. The police soon had me in cuffs, and he was still laying on the floor as they whisked me off to lockup, a smile on my face the whole trip. I was later asked if I regretted my actions that day, and I said yes. I wish I had eaten the pizza first.

## Chapter 21
## Alone Again

J.P.R.U. doesn't have a lockup; it's a minimum security and pre-release jail, so if you mess up, they throw you in a van and take you to the check-in jail, the notorious Brockbridge. Brockbridge Correctional Facility in the early '90s was a death camp. It was flawed from the beginning. They house you there till a bed opens in medium or maximum security, but it also houses people who have done well and are waiting for a bed in minimum or pre-release. The big brains seem not to notice that this creates an institution where guys who have nothing to lose are able to prey on those that have everything to lose! To compound the problem, the jail is wide open. When they open the doors for recreation or chow, they release five dorms downstairs and six dorms upstairs. You have 1,500 guys running all over the place.

People get stuck up for their commissary in the stairwell on a regular basis. There are so many assaults and stabbings it's like living in the projects. The difference is you have some law-abiding citizens in the projects. Not so at BCF! I was on the lockup tier for thirty days before they turned me over to gen pop. I knew what I had to do, and I set about doing it right away. On my first morning, I watched a dude get beaten by six other men with locks in socks. They put heavy locks intended to secure your locker inside socks that are reinforced with dental floss so they won't break as easily and use them to beat someone. This particular guy had stuck up someone on the street, and that someone happened to have a family member at BCF. The stick-up kid was there less than twenty-four hours when six guys surrounded his bed while he was sleeping. They knocked his teeth out and broke the bones in his face and around his eyes. A helicopter landed in the yard and flew him to shock trauma. Most inmates weren't upset that a man had been beaten; they were angry that the helicopter forced the yard to close and interrupted their workout. It was a brutal jail!!

What I'm about to say is just a simple fact. If you think I'm a racist, that's up to you, but I know what the Maryland prison system is like. White guys are the minority in prison; they are outnumbered 10 to 1 and are therefore victimized quite often. I knew that strength came in numbers, and I knew the white guys were ripe for assembly. There was a guy I knew indirectly because he had did time with my brother. His nickname was "Chief," and everybody called him that. We set about putting a crew together of strong white dudes and even some not-so-strong white dudes. We let it be known that if you messed with one, the rest were coming for you. I would list the guys by name, but I'm not sure where some of them are today, and I don't know if they want their name associated with prison life. I know many of them are dead and at least two of them are big in the notorious prison gang Dead Man Incorporated, which was started by a childhood friend of mine Perry Roark (look for my next book)! Anyway, my crew was solid, and we had crazy respect from everyone. If the stick-up boys wanted to rob a white guy, they would approach us and ask if that guy was on our team. With a nod of my head, I could stop an assault or robbery. Or I could turn your lights out!

Drugs, however, would mess up that whole crew, as well. They had enough of my antics in the visiting room and had taken my visits away for six months. So I had to get creative. I had a girl go to my mom and pick up the dope, and she would deliver it to a guy I grew up with. So I was running dope through Brockbridge and started using so much I developed a jailhouse habit. When I would run out, I'd go to other dealers, who would gladly front me till I got my shipment. There was a lieutenant trying to bust me at every turn and there was a continual cat-and-mouse game between him and me. I was forty days away from flattening my sentence when the bottom fell out of my operation.

I was a few hundred in debt to the black drug dealers. The lieutenant transferred six guys from my crew to other jails and put two more on administrative seg (which is when you get put on lockup while they investigate you so you can be locked up indefinitely). Then he busted my boy who was bringing the dope in for me. They locked the girl up in the parking lot and sent my friend to maximum security that night!

So here's my position: I'm in debt to some badass dudes, my crew is gone, there's me and my number two guy Chief, and he's about to be transferred any day. Everyone is gone in one way or another, and I'm no longer dealing from a position of strength. I didn't like my chances, but I had to go talk to the dope dealer and explain I needed a few days to come up with their money. When the door hit, I went upstairs and headed straight to the dude. I told him what happened. He assured me he had heard about the girl getting busted and figured I'd be in a little bit of a jam. He said it was cool, and I could pay a little at a time. I walked away knowing something was wrong. This guy had people jumped over ten dollars, but here he was acting as if a few hundred were no big deal. My survivor senses were on high when I hit my dorm. Chief was approaching fast. "Look, man, you gotta go on protective custody. My transfer is tomorrow and there's a hit on you."

I let his words sink in. "I'll be okay; don't worry about it." I smiled while I lied.

I knew the seriousness of my situation, but I just didn't know what to do. I was at the end of my sentence, but I had to make it through this or I'd never taste freedom. As I was standing there, a correctional officer walked up and said, "Fred, the L.T. wants you immediately." *Man*, I thought, *things just keep getting better and better*.

I walked down the tier toward the area known as Traffic, where the offices and the main hub of the jail were. I knew this was bad when the lieutenant took me in an empty office. "There's a hit on you," he said right away. No pleasantries, just the facts. This guy was all business, but I saw sincere concern in his eyes.

I smiled my big tough guy smile, not allowing fear to show, a said, "Boy, good news travels fast."

"I can offer you protective custody," he countered, as if I hadn't spoken.

"Thanks, lieutenant, but I'll be OK. I've been getting killed for a long time. I only have to survive thirty-five days or so before I go home." I tried to sound as if I weren't at all concerned, but inside, my thoughts were racing and my stomach was in knots.

"I figured you'd say that. You're free to go," he said as I stood up and headed for the door.

I was headed back to my dorm, and I had many eyes on me. Most figured I'd check in to P.C. Word spread fast that I refused to check in. I had people I had helped out of one jam or another trying not to look at me. I was afraid and watching everyone. I knew they would try to sneak up on me, so I kept my awareness on full blast, as I tried to look like I was going about business as usual. I walked to my bunk, where I saw two guys come in my dorm, look at me and head to the bathroom. One thing I know is its not coming from where I expect it; they will get my attention in one area, and then hit me from another. Two more of the dope dealer's crew come in my dorm and go in the bathroom. I know they're assembling to come at me. A straightforward attack is unusual, but not unheard of. I grabbed a shank from under my mattress and started walking toward the bathroom. As I start through the door, I hear the main door open. Two correctional officers walk in. I dump the shank and head back toward my bunk.

The two guards are on me. "Slow your roll, Fred, you're going to lockup!"

## Chapter 22
## Dream Police

I've never been so happy to feel cuffs go on my wrists. They took me to lockup and told me they were putting me on administrative segregation pending investigation. That means they can lock you up for an indefinite amount of time while they investigate you for whatever reason. In my case, the paperwork said I was a violent drug runner, but in truth, the lieutenant knew I was too proud to go on PC, so he cooked the paperwork to lock me up till I went home. I was minutes from a kill-or-be-killed situation, and I'm thankful that guard locked me up. I finished up four years, four months and fifteen days on a five-year sentence and was released from segregation. It was the middle of 1995, and I had the world in front of me.

I walked out weighing 205 lbs. and carrying 8% body fat. I had a great build and a terrible attitude. It never occurred to me that I had done the maximum amount on my sentence and that I was released from lockup, so maybe I wasn't ready for the street. The world wasn't ready for me, but more importantly I wasn't ready for it. About nine months before my release, I had started talking to a girl named Joan. She wasn't my type with thick glasses and a little on the heavy side, but out of some sense of loyalty to her for writing me and sending me money, I let her be my girlfriend. What a mistake that was. I had no idea what trouble she was, but I was about to find out.

At first, things were cool. My older brother Steve had made parole about a year before my release date. We had always had a rocky relationship, but like I said earlier, I looked up to him for all the wrong reasons.

My first day out was pretty quiet. My mom was sick and went straight to bed after I walked in. My father had set it up so that the house went in my name upon his death, so my mother wanted me to take a loan to get myself started. She had a habit again. I swear I just couldn't get a break. The girl Joan came over and we had sex. Any sex is pretty good after four years without it, but I knew we just weren't compatible in that area. She left and a girl from the neighborhood I'd known for years stopped by. I made it seem like I hadn't been with anyone in over four years, and even though she had a boyfriend, we had sex. She was more my speed, curvy with a flat belly and an appetite that matched my own. She told me to say the word, and she would break it off with the boyfriend, but I had to stay away from drugs and other women. It was then that I told her about the girl Joan and how I felt a sense of loyalty to her for writing me and sending me packages and money while I was in the can. I often wonder what would have happened if I had made a different choice that night.

My second day was trouble on the way. My brother stopped by and introduced me to his friend, Robert. Steve had lost about 40 lbs. in the past year and looked terrible. Robert had a connection for some really strong heroin. Needless to say I would go on to be fast friends with Robert. Steve and I talked, and he admitted to sending the guy to see me at The New Jail and laughed when I told him how it all unfolded. We agreed to meet the next day. He went home with his girlfriend, and boy, would he be sorry he ever met her. Remember the junkie girl who got my mom hooked on smack? Well, it was her. A relationship made in hell! I sent Robert to get me some dope and went home to get high. The girl Joan showed up, and it was easier to be with her once I was loaded on heroin. I should have just broken it off, but I couldn't.

The next morning, I got word they had surrounded the house my brother was staying in and locked him up on a parole violation. I'll never know the truth of that whole deal. The girl told me one thing, my brother told me another, and I suppose the truth falls somewhere in between. The end of the story is that my brother went back to jail for another few years. Parole would hear his case in another three years to see if he deserved another chance. I guess we just weren't meant to hang out 'cause we only had a few hours of freedom together. So many things remained unspoken between us. I didn't know it then, but it would be years before we ever really talked about things that were important to us, but I'll get to that later on.

I started getting high with the black dude, Robert, that my brother introduced me to. He was my kind of people. He had great connections and would snort some dope with me, but he never touched needles and always went home to his girl at 7:00 p.m., no matter what was going on. I respected his lifestyle. I mean, he got high, but he did it in moderation, and he loved his girl and their little boy. By now, you know my story. I started doing a little dope, it swings out of control, and next thing ya know I'm robbing and stealing and heading to the penitentiary! Well, this won't be much different, but things would change this time around in a big way. I would have access to more drugs than ever, and I would straddle the thinnest of lines between life and death. It is only by the grace of God that I am here today to tell the story.

So as you go to the next chapter, I want you to get a cup

of coffee, light up a cigarette and put on a seatbelt, 'cause my addictions are about to go into high gear, and when traveling at those breakneck speeds, the crash is a few things: imminent, destructive and horrific! I couldn't see it, and you couldn't warn me. I had to live it, but maybe, just maybe, you won't have to. Read on.

## Chapter 23
## Paradise City

After my father's death the house was in mine and my mother's name. My mother wanted me to take a loan on the house, and I was running out of options. I tried working, but I had a lot of trouble finding a job, and then when I did, my addictions would screw it up. I was caught up in being the man of the house and taking care of my mother, but in all honesty, I was a dumb kid who couldn't manage a paper route. I had no idea how to make money work for me, other than sell drugs. I had watched my father get moderately wealthy from little yellow pills, so why couldn't I? But times were changing. While I was in the can, a new drug had taken over. Crack cocaine was the big drug on the street, and it was everywhere. People who had never touched drugs when I went to prison were strung out on this drug when I came home.

So I took a loan on the house and started selling crack. Of course, the whole time I was selling, I was using heroin and watching my girlfriend smoke up as much crack as she cooked. I even joined in and smoked with her, but my first love was heroin. Even with us using lots of drugs, I was still turning a profit, so I brought my lifelong friend Chris into the mix. (Chris deserves his own chapter in this book, but I just don't have the room. Nonetheless, let me tell you a little bit about him. I asked him to write the foreword to this book because I don't think anyone on the planet knows me better. We started out as less than friends—when I was about eight years old, he hit me in the nose with a snowball. If you had told me then that we would be lifelong friends, I would have laughed. Today, Chris is more than a friend he's my brother. He has been around me my whole life and has never crossed me or did me wrong. I can honestly say I love the guy and would do anything for him. When we were teenagers partying and getting high, he was one of the few people who could handle my ego. We never had a fight, and I'm glad of it 'cause I'm sure he would have won, but I'm also glad because I'm one of a few who can say I have a friend I can trust with anything.)

I was a little jealous of Chris 'cause he had those surfer good looks and all the girls went crazy when he walked in. He has a quiet calm about him that I really respected, and let me tell you something, he may be quiet and calm, but if you break his peace and make him angry, you got your hands full. He's one of the most ferocious fighters I've ever seen and one of the best athletes. To say I hold him in high regard is an understatement. I brought him into the crack selling deal and by this time he was smoking it, too, but even still we continued to make a profit. Joan would cook up the powder into rock cocaine, then she'd bag it up. I'd take the call and Chris would make the delivery and collect the cash. I had two pagers jumping 24 hours a day. I was driving rental cars and acting like a mafia godfather. When I wasn't so stoned out on heroin and crack to say my name, I was a big shot.

There were lots of parties and drug-fueled nights. I had lots of people around me, but only Chris was my friend. He started to back away as the scene got crazier, and I don't blame him. I started to lose money as the drugs took over.

It wasn't a sudden fall, just a steady decline. There were nights where I was so high on cocaine I was locked in my bathroom with guns, drugs and money, just convinced the cops or whoever were coming to get me. On other nights, I was the life of the party, passing out drugs and holding court in my father's kitchen, inches from the spot where he had taken his last breath. I was the one with the money and drugs, so I was king of my small world, but heavy is the head that wears the crown. No one can sustain that lifestyle, and mine was fading fast. I was losing money on every package because of the parties and my use. The deadline to start paying the loan back was drawing near, but I was hardly thinking about that.

Actually, I wasn't thinking about much at all. I would party for three or four days with no sleep, then crash and burn, sleeping 18-24 hours, only rising to use the bathroom. I was losing customers because of my inconsistency. The one thing a drug user wants is his dealer to answer the phone and deliver the drugs fast. I was falling apart, yelling at my customers and making them wait till I was ready. I'd have to wake up around midnight and shoot three caps of heroin before I was ready to do business at 1:30 a.m., and then I'd sell crack and shoot speedballs, drinking and having sex in between. Lots of females were throwing themselves at me, and I was getting to the point where I didn't care if Joan found out. I would give her some crack and send her upstairs, and I'd be downstairs getting a blowjob. At one point, a guy offered his wife to me when they ran out of money, and I wouldn't give them more credit. He sat at my kitchen table smoking coke while she performed fellatio in the living room. It was one crazy, drug-fueled scene after the next.

My one true friend had stopped coming around, so I was surrounded by fake friends telling me how wonderful I was while things were getting worse by the day. On one occasion, I was taking a break, just selling and not having a bunch of people over. My mother was staying at my sister's house, so on this night, it was just me and Joan at the house watching a movie, when a guy named Dave stopped by to buy some rock. He asked if he could do a hit there at the house. I said yes and walked away, but as I sat down, I saw him trying to get Joan's attention. Even though I wasn't attracted to her, she was with me, so that meant hands off. I'm not sure why it was out, but there was one of those old-style soldering guns on the counter, and before I thought about it, I was beating Dave in the head and face with the heavy metal object. Blood was flying and he was trying to get out the door, but I always put the deadbolt on when someone came to buy something. The soldering gun broke and it brought me out of my rage. Dave was begging me to stop, and as I looked at him, I saw how tore up he was. He was bleeding from numerous places on his head and face. I had Joan get a towel and help him clean up. I knew things were bad. If he ran to the cops I was going back to the joint for a long time.

As she cleaned him up, I sat there thinking about what I could do. I didn't want him running to the police, but something crazy was about to take place. He came over and started apologizing to me, "I'm sorry Freddie Jay. Sometimes I don't think straight after I take a hit. I didn't mean to disrespect you or your girl."

I just looked at him. I was about to give him some dope and offer to pay for a doctor's visit, but as he apologized, I decided to play a different card. "Look, Dave, I'm sorry you made me do this, but I'm willing to forget it if you are. Just tell people you had a car accident or something, and I won't tell anyone how you acted here tonight." He readily agreed and I gave him a twenty-dollar piece of coke and let him out the door. I never saw him after that, which was fine by me.

As another night turned into morning, I knew my life was on the verge of collapse. I laid in bed with an overwhelming feeling of impending doom. I felt like a lost little boy, and I had absolutely no one to turn to. I was Frankenstein's monster, put together with pieces of lies, half truths, all things ugly and all things narcotic! The train wreck that was my life was coming off the tracks. I had created a perverse merry-go-round that was spinning out of control, and I was unable to get off! I wanted so badly to be rescued, to be saved from myself, but there was nothing or no one to turn to. I had ostracized myself from anyone who cared even a little. The only people around me fed the monster 'cause they wanted a piece of the monster. There was only one thing to do—I picked an argument with Joan and she left. I was completely alone without a friend in the world. I sat on the floor and cooked up the biggest shot of heroin I could fit into a syringe. I ejected the drug and prayed it would end my misery, but I couldn't even get that right. I sat there and nodded in and out of consciousness, smoking cigarettes and slobbering on myself. This was my world. Welcome to paradise!!

Chapter 24
The Needle and the Damage Done

Before long I was totally broke. You just can't use drugs and sell at the same time. It works for awhile, but it always ends with your habit out of control. The parties ended, people stopped coming around, the loan was due and I was strung out with a huge habit. I started selling things out of the house. I basically sold anything of value to maintain my drug habit. My mother was in Delaware asking me to sell the house and split the money with her before they foreclosed and we got nothing. I knew the house was going and in some ways, I wanted it to go. There was so much pain and ugliness in that house, it represented all the things I had become and I hated it. I blamed my father for my life; I blamed my mother, the police, the courts, the prison system, the dope dealers and everyone and everything except the person I should have blamed—me!

Truth is, I hated myself, loathed my station in life and believed I was destined for failure, jails, institutions and death! I wanted to kill myself, but I was too much of a coward to pull the trigger. Hell, if you handed me a gun, I'd sell it to do more dope. My life was at an extreme low. I really thought I couldn't sink any lower, but I was wrong. I had an acquaintance who knew a guy who knew a guy who would buy the house, so introductions were made. This guy thought he was going to assume the loan and me walk away. I told him I'd burn it to the ground first, and I meant it from the bottom of my heart. It was a row home and I knew I wasn't going to get rich, but I wanted to walk away with a little something. So the legal wrangling began. After loans were paid and lawyers fees, closing cost and God only knows what other fees, I walked away with twelve thousand in cash.

I had good intensions, I thought about opening a pizzeria or a newsstand, something to generate a little living for myself, but the truth is, I was too strung out to make any kind of good decisions. So I went to a motel, where I did heroin and cocaine till I was out of my mind. After about a week and a half, I finally called my mother at my sister's house. I had already pissed through a few thousand. It would have been bad enough by myself, but I had Joan there and a couple that were half-assed friends. I got them a room and we got stoned for a week, with me paying for everything, of course. I was ready for the guy to take his big-mouthed girl and go, but they didn't want to leave the free ride. I called my mother looking for help. If she had told me she was coming to get me to go to rehab, I would have gone, but she was interested in only one thing: money! I tried to ask for help. I knew the money was going, and I was going to be on the street. I needed a plan; I needed a mother. Then my mother, who was claiming to be sick, talking to me in her sick voice, suddenly got better when I told her I would come by the next day to give her some money. Her graveled voice suddenly turned to honey and when I called her on it, she suddenly returned to her "sick voice."

I got off the phone and sent the guy and his girl along with Joan to go get dope and coke. While they were gone, I took the money and hid it behind the drywall in the room, and I sat on the bed and cried like a baby. I cried like I hadn't cried in years. I had this money, but it wouldn't last, the relationship with Joan was a joke, and the couple were only there to suck up as many drugs as they could. I was alone, the house was gone and to top it off, my mother tried to use my love for her against me. I thought about all the trips to the hospital as a kid, going with my mom to her chemo treatments and cobalt treatments. I loved my mother more than anyone, and she had abandoned me when times got tough. I was incapable of looking at my part in all this. I had become the worst kind of junkie. I had sold my mother's house, and now I was blaming her for it. The addicted mind is a minefield at best, but mine was headed to the point of no return.

I rented a house in Essex, Maryland. I had a rented vehicle, and I was tearing through the money. It was an aimless existence and the end was coming. It wouldn't be long till I was in stores stealing to support my habit. The money gone, the-so called friends gone, my family gone. The relationship with Joan ended when I lost the house in Essex, although it was over long before. We stayed together just to blame each other for our sorry lives. Little did I know it would be an infection in my leg that would save my life. I was basically living on the streets, stealing to get my daily drugs, sleeping where I could and living like an animal. My bodybuilder's frame had shrunk down to 151 lbs., my cheeks were hollow and I looked like a skeleton. I had cut my leg jumping a security fence to sleep in an abandoned trailer. I didn't think much of it; I was just getting somewhere warm to sleep, and it didn't hurt much at that moment.

A week or so later, my leg really started hurting. I could see it was getting infected, but I didn't have time to worry about that. I had to get to the stores, steal enough stuff to sell in the bars on the way to get my dope. I went in one of those mega-pharmacies, you know the kind where you drop off a prescription, get your watch battery replaced, and develop your photos while they rotate your tires. I grabbed three cameras and a cordless phone; this would bring me a quick hundred from the Greeks in the coffee shop who bought my stolen goods for pennies on the dollar. I slipped the items into my backpack when I noticed this guy one aisle over watching me through the mirror. Once you put the stuff in a bag you stole it; it's called theft by concealment. Since I had already committed to it, I headed for the door. I saw the guy headed for me, and I started running. I got outside, made a quick left and was headed for the wooded area behind the store. Thinking the guy never came out of the store, I slowed a little, my leg throbbing and my out-of-shape lungs ready to burst!

It was only then that I heard the footsteps behind me. In the next instance, the guy tackled me, and we both went rolling into the hedgerow, where the wooded area began. I came up on my feet and turned to square off with the guy. Only then did I realize it was two of them, but a junkie will fight till the death not to go to jail. It's pure torture kicking a dope habit in the county lockup. When the guy saw my posture, he knew they had a fight coming. "Hold on, dude, hold on. Just let me talk to you," the one guy was saying as the other tried to circle behind me. I grabbed a broken tree branch off the ground and let him know that tactic wasn't working. The first guy told his buddy to back off. The guy reluctantly backed off and even walked maybe 20 feet away. You could see he wanted to take me down, but he obeyed his boss. So the guy says, "Look, we don't want to call police, but if you give us the camera back, we will write a report. You won't be allowed back in the store but you'll be free to go."

I said, "I'll give you the camera, but I'm not going back

in the store with you."

The guy knew he had a cornered animal that would fight tooth and nail not to go peacefully. "OK, give me the camera." He told his buddy to go back to the store and make sure the cashier hadn't called the police. Again, the second guy reluctantly obeyed. So the other guy asks me if I have a drug habit and tells me about his brother being on heroin. I hand him one camera and to this day I believe that man knew I had two more cameras and a cordless phone in my bag. Then the guy does two of the most bizarre things I had ever seen. He reaches in his pocket and pulls out forty bucks he says, "I'll give you this if you let me pray with you."

I said, "Sure, let's pray," but inside I'm concerned this guy is stalling till the cops get there.

He looks me dead in the eye and as if he's reading my thoughts, says "No cops are coming." I just looked at him and tears of shame streamed down my dirty face. He put his hand on my shoulder and began to pray. Tears flowed as he covered me in the blood of Jesus even though I had no understanding of what that meant at the time. He prayed for five minutes and I cried for five minutes, and after he said "amen," he handed me the money. He then said three words that would ring over and over in my head. He smiled and said, "Go in peace."

I turned and headed through the woods with those words bouncing around in my head.

## Chapter 25
## Winds of Change

    I went to the coffee shops and sold my stolen items. I was happy because I made enough to hold me for a few days. I tucked some money in my shoe and went to cop my drugs. After getting my dope, I went into an abandoned house to shoot up. As I pulled the syringe out of my arm and that feeling I risked my life for was flooding through me, I had a moment of absolute clarity. In that instant I saw the filth I was wallowing in. I saw the empty bags and discarded needles at my feet and I heard Satan's laughter. I saw a sheet being pulled over my face and heard my mother crying. Some would say I had a vision, but at that moment I was so scared of what I was seeing, but as fear flooded my brain and the heroin took over, the clarity was gone. I sat down on the floor and a girl came in to shoot up. I watched her go through her ritual as I nodded in and out. The whole time I kept hearing these words, "Go in peace."
    After some time had passed, I found myself talking to the girl and she asked me where I was staying. I told her I was on the streets and didn't know where I was getting shot money in the morning. I had money in my shoe, but I wasn't about to tell her that. Junkie girls are a devious lot, and I've seen them set guys up who were supposed to know

the game. Anyway, this girl, her name was Amber—or at least that was the name she was using.—told me she had a motel room that I could come stay at but when a trick showed up I had to take a walk. This girl turned out to be a hooker with a heart of gold. I went to the motel with her, but I was still wary of this little skinny girl. When you're on the street, everyone is out for themselves. It's a dangerous dirty little world. When I took a shower, I took my money in with me. I washed my socks and underwear and put them over the heat vent to dry. I crawled into bed and was out like a light.

The next morning, she handed me $100 and told me what to get. I couldn't believe she was trusting me, but she was, and I went straight to the dope man and back to the room. After we got high, she said she had a business proposition for me. Sometimes her tricks got violent or didn't want to pay, and if I would be her security guy, she would hook me up daily and we'd have adjoining rooms. So I wasn't sure how much money this mousy-lookin' girl could make, but I agreed, and man, was I shocked at how much money she made. I never realized how many desperate dudes there were, but it wouldn't be long before I would be earning my keep.

That afternoon, she got me the room next to hers. A couple guys had been there, did their thing and left. I was thinking this was gonna be an easy job, but I soon found out how wrong I was.

As I said, we had adjoining rooms, so when a dude would show up, I'd walk over, get the money from him, then I'd go over to my room leaving the door separating our rooms ajar. After they got done, I'd walk over and check on her, then either shoot dope or go buy more or whatever. So after this older guy left, I was getting ready to go to the sub shop and get us some sandwiches, but Amber asked me to stay. She said this guy was coming and he had got her number from one of her regulars, but she wasn't sure about him.

I agreed. After all, this was what she was paying me to do. I didn't like the guy as soon as she opened the door to let him in. I don't know why, but I picked up her room key off the desk in her room and slipped it in my pocket. They negotiated, and while he didn't like giving me the money, he did and I headed for my room. He said, "Hey, can you close that door?"

I said, "The door must stay cracked for her safety, but I'll be watching TV, so go ahead and enjoy yourself. But leave the door open." I could see he didn't like my answer, but the truth is, I couldn't stand those slimeballs and was waiting for my chance to beat one of them up.

I walked into my room and turned my TV up. I hated to hear the disgusting sounds these men made. I wasn't sure as to why I hated the men who used the services of hookers so much, but I guess it made me think of the things my mother endured when she was a hooker. I imagine a therapist could have a field day digging around in my head about those sorts of things.

I had just lit a cigarette when I thought I heard Amber yell my name. I headed toward the door to double check, but as I got closer, I heard the dude cussing. Amber screamed and as I reached for the door, he slammed and locked it. Instead of trying to open the door, I went straight out my main door, fishing her door key out of my pocket. I opened her main door. The man was still pressed up against the adjoining doors holding amber by the hair. He was naked from the waist down, and you should have seen the terror in his eyes when I came through the door he thought was locked up tight. I grabbed a small brass lamp and started for him. He released Amber immediately as I closed in. He threw his hands up to shield his face, but I was already swinging the lamp. I caught him in the side of the head, and he buckled straight to the ground. I dropped the lamp and threw a volley of lefts and rights to his head. I stepped back, and as he looked up, I kicked him square is the face. His head snapped back and out went the lights as he hit the ground, knocked out cold!

I turned to look at Amber, who was crying her eyes out. In that moment I didn't see the street-tough hooker; I saw a scared little girl. My leg was throbbing from the fight. By now I had a high-grade infection from not taking care of myself properly. I found out that the problem started because the guy didn't want to wear a condom. This amazed me that a guy using the services of a hooker wouldn't want to use a condom, but that's what started the trouble. I got her settled was nicer to her than I ever had been, and she took it wrong. She tried to kiss me, and while I was a junkie, I prided myself on being a clean junkie. Kissing a girl who performed fellatio for twenty five bucks is something I wasn't about to do. I quickly brushed it off, but the damage was done.

I went and got some drugs, but when I got back, my leg was hurting worse than ever. Amber took a look at it and told me I needed to go to the hospital. We acted like nothing happened, but there was an uneasiness between us now that had never been there before. For some reason, I stashed forty dollars in cash and five capsules of some very powerful heroin in my shower bag. It's a good thing, too, because changes were coming fast.

## Chapter 26
## Under the Bridge

I knew that guarding a hooker wasn't a career, but I never dreamed it would end so abruptly. I woke up and walked over to her room. I knocked and no one answered. That wasn't unusual. She would get up early and go cop our dope some mornings. There's nothing better for a junkie then waking up to your morning shot. I went back to my room and jumped in the shower. I got out and was getting dressed when a knock came to the door. My leg was killing me as I hobbled over to let Amber in. To my surprise, it was the guy from the motel office. "Will you be checking out today?" he asked with a polite smile.

I said, "Gimme a break, man. She should be back soon, and she will come up to pay for our rooms."

He looked at me quizzically and said, "She checked out at 7:00 a.m. We were surprised, too. She's been here for months."

I felt foolish and my face reddened. "Oh, that's right. Yes, I'll be meeting her later today. Yes, I'll check out today. Just give me an hour to get things together." I lied unconvincingly as he just turned to walk away.

I stepped back in the room and was furious. Who did this little whore think she was? If she was dipping out 'cause I wouldn't kiss a professional dick sucker, well then, good riddance. What the hell should I do now? My mind scrambled, but first things first. I dug two capsules of dope out of my shower bag and blasted off. I packed up my little gym bag, and even though the heroin was strong, I was in a lot of pain. I knew I couldn't walk far on this leg, let alone hit the streets again, but what choice did I have? I headed out and caught a ride with a girl who lived in the motel. She dropped me off in town. I had a grand total of, like, sixty five bucks and a few caps of heroin. I stopped by my black girl's house and she was always happy to see me, but her house was too crazy for me. I only went there when I wanted to shoot up or to have sex with her. I could have moved right in, but she had a brother that hated me, and he always had his friends running in and out and there was a constant threat in the air. He and I had squared off to fight one day, and he pulled a gun. His sister stepped in between us or I believe he would have shot me. Anyway, the more of his friends that showed up, the braver he got, and the insults or racial jokes would get more pointed till I finally left.

Tamika took one look at my leg and told me I had to get to the hospital. We stayed in her room that night and the next morning I bought some dope that was relatively weak for what I was use to, shot up and headed for Baltimore City Hospital. I went to the emergency room and sat there for hours. My dope was beginning to wear off and my leg was absolutely on fire. They called my name, and I headed for the examination room. After some preliminaries, they put me in a robe and I sat on a cold chair waiting for the doctor to come in. After an eternity, he came in and looked at my leg and without any further examination said something that scared the hell out of me. "I hope we can save the leg. You have a very serious infection." He then said something to the nurse that cheered me up. "Demerol, stat."

I was in the hospital for eight days and the doctor in charge of my case was a great guy who, for some reason, I told the truth, I admitted I was homeless, that I was a dope addict, that I had no insurance and this doctor still treated me with kindness and respect. They got me a social worker who got me insurance and found a shelter in the county for me to go to. They filled my prescriptions in the hospital and overall treated me great. While I was there, they pumped me full of very expensive antibiotics and at one point, cut my leg open. As I got better, I would get in my wheelchair and go downstairs to bum cigarettes. One night I asked a lady who was smoking if I could have a cigarette. She looked at me like I was scum and said, "Why doesn't your family bring you cigarettes?" I wheeled away without a response I had gotten use to being the world's whipping post.

I asked another guy who wouldn't even acknowledge my existence. I started to roll back in when the first woman walked back over to me. "I'm sorry I was short with you. My son had a stroke, and I'm not myself." As she spoke, she handed me two cigarettes, which I accepted with a smile. We made small talk and I told her why I was in the hospital, then lied about my family living out of state. I crushed out a cigarette and rolled back up to my room thinking she was an odd bird, but nice just the same. I was shocked when she walked in my room the next day. She brought me soap, shampoo, cigarettes and a twenty dollar bill. I was surprised by her kindness. We went downstairs to have a smoke and as we were talking, she asked me if I knew Jesus. I didn't know how to answer her. I had the guy from the store (his words had echoed in my ears for days— "Go in peace"), and I had a crush on a girl when I was a teenager who took me to church. I even attended church with my next-door neighbors when I was very small, but did I know Jesus?

I had a general idea of who Jesus was, but no, I didn't know Him. As she told me about the Gospel and left me with something to read, I was lost in my thoughts. I remembered being a child and going to a little church with my neighbors. After we went in the little white church where the preacher would speak of a loving father, we would go to my friend's grandmother's house. She had a big back yard where we would play football with the adults and then sit down to a big lunch, fried chicken, cornbread, and baked beans with lots of brown sugar. The adults would laugh and occasionally yell at Johnny and me for misbehaving, but I never felt threatened there. Mr. John was a big man, but he never said much to me. He knew my father was a crazy man and I think he felt bad for me, but he never wanted to yell at me to the point that I ran to my dad. Mrs. Nancy was a wonderful woman who always had a smile for me. Those memories were some of the only good memories when I was a child. It was a brief vacation and then it was back to hell.

You may think this is the part of the book where I find Jesus and everything turns to sunshine, but that would be too easy. So please don't stop reading— there's much more to come!

## Chapter 27
## Seasons of Wither

The truth is, I prayed to Jesus and asked him to come into my life and miraculous changes did come about, but it was the beginning. God had much work to do in my damaged soul, and I didn't make it easy. I made Him work for it. I would spend the next few years running from the inevitable, but let's stick to the narrative.

I wouldn't print the lady's name anyway, but honestly, I don't remember her name. I do remember praying with her and tears streaming down my face. I was a man with a broken heart and a broken soul, and it's through those breaks that God would find his way in. Again He had his work cut out, but it was a start, a beginning of a total change. Little did I know that it would be another ten years before I fully submitted. At that time, I truly believed that Jesus was magic, and that after praying, my life would get instantly better with the wave of God's magic wand. I had a lot to learn, but let me tell you things started happening that were amazing, and I must give God the credit for turning my life around—and I could've kept it if I had stayed grateful!

A social worker came to my room and asked me where I was going when I left the hospital. I could have given her any of ten addresses where I had mail sent, but for some reason I told her the truth. "I don't have anywhere to go. I'm a heroin addict who just got clean. I stole from my friends and family and no one wants me around, so when I go out that door, I go to the streets."

The lady sat there searching my eyes, looking for signs of yanking her. After a full minute of silence, she stood and walked out of the room without a word. I felt good for some reason. I mean it was obvious she wasn't going to help, but I felt good about telling the truth. Heroin addicts lie so much that we forget which lie we told last, and why do we lie? Most of the time we are manipulating someone for money, drugs or sex. It becomes second nature when you're living that life. I have lied and then thought to myself, why? Why did you lie when the truth would've worked, but it's all part of the lifestyle. We also lie out of shame. We don't want people to see the real person, so we build grand stories and hide behind half truths and outright lies.

The doctors came in with what they thought was good news. I was being released in the morning. I smiled and thanked them, but as they left the room, despair filled my mind. Where would I go? I wanted to stay off of drugs, but everywhere I could go was built around a drug relationship. My heart ached, and here's the funny thing—I had stopped taking my pain medicine, saving every dose they brought me. The biggest fear a junkie has is being sick, so saving pills was my safety net. In a way, they had detoxed me in the hospital. I came in on heroin and they put me on Demerol, then moved me down to Dilaudid and Percocet, and then down further to Tylox. I took myself off Tylox with only minor discomfort. The next morning, the doctors came in all happy. Today was discharge day and most patients were overjoyed to return to their loved ones, but me, I had nothing. I signed the papers and they gave me some prescriptions to take with me. As the doctors left, the social worker came in.

Good morning, Frederick. Come with me." I followed her to the elevator without a word. I figured I had more papers to sign. We got off the elevator, and she took me to this window and said, "This is the pharmacy. They'll fill your prescription." I looked at the floor and admitted I didn't have money to pay for them. She smiled and said, "We will take care of it." I was shocked. I gushed my thanks, and she just smiled.

They handed me my prescription s in under ten minutes, and I followed the social worker to her office. "I've arranged for you to go to a shelter," she said. I started to balk. I knew the Baltimore city shelters were worse than some of the Baltimore prisons, but she held up a hand. "This is a small place out in the county that is run by a church. It's not what you're thinking. In fact, they only accept certain people, and you must have a referral from a church member."

I stared at her, until it dawned on me she was the church member giving me the referral. But why? After a short silence, she spoke. "I went home last night, and I couldn't get you off my mind. I prayed and prayed and I came to work an hour early today to make sure you didn't go to the streets. You can return the favor by doing well in this program." Tears streamed down my face. Here was undeniable proof that God was working on my behalf—not because I deserved it, but because He loved me. I thanked her over and over and asked her how to get there. She smiled again. "A cab has been paid for you and is waiting."

I walked out of the hospital in shock. I couldn't believe all the things suddenly going in my favor. I arrived at the shelter and was convinced it was the wrong place. It was a long driveway to a big white house, with another big house behind it. I got out of the cab and two guys hustled out.

"Hey, Fred, welcome to Nehemiah House." They grabbed my little bag for me and showed me to the office. I met with the guy who ran the place and soon was shown to my sleeping area. It was a room with four bunk beds all made with military precision. There was a TV room and a game room and everyone I met had a smile. I fell into a routine quickly at Nehemiah House. I did all that was asked of me and more. I attended Bible study and church and found camaraderie with the other guys there. I got my ID and a Social Security card. My leg was healing nicely and things were looking up.

    I felt I was finally on the right road. My life was going great. I was offered drugs and turned them down. I saw people come back in under the influence and stood strong. I was ready to take on the world; I felt like Superman.

    Across the street from Nehemiah House was the Golden Ring Mall. When I was bored I'd go over, get a soft pretzel and watch girls. So one night, my new buddy Gus and I walked over to the mall and there she stood shopping at a perfume kiosk in the middle of the mall. She was five foot and maybe a hundred and ten pounds with eyes the color of ice. She had black curls that hung loose down to her tight butt. Ladies and gentlemen, meet Kryptonite!!

## Chapter 28
## Pocketful of Kryptonite

I walked over to her and although it sounds corny now, I thought it was pretty good at the time. "Excuse me, miss, but you should let me help you pick out the perfect perfume. I mean, we are going to be spending a lot of time together, and I think it should be a fragrance I like as well as you."

A slow smile spread across her face. "Well, that's original," she said in a melodic voice. We made introductions and went upstairs to have a hamburger. I could barely afford it. I had made money taking surveys in the mall, and it didn't pay that well. She was easy to talk to and seemed to really like me. Her name was Melissa. She worked as a legal secretary for a big law firm and had a nine-year-old son from a former relationship. We talked and talked. I gave her total disclosure. I wanted all my cards on the table, but she left out one small detail about herself.

She drove me back to the shelter that night and laid a serious kiss on me. I knew she wanted me to think about that kiss long after she left, and I did. Quite a bit, in fact. I can't say I was in love, but I was smitten with this tiny girl. She seemed so perfect. She had her life together, her own place and a great job. She was a good citizen, something I had never been, but desperately wanted to be. I wanted respect from my peers, love and admiration from my lady and a family to share life's ups and downs! I desperately wanted a son to make up for not being a father to my first born. Our relationship took off. We went to museums and concerts where she taught me about art and refined things. When we went to dinner, she knew the perfect wine (not that I could drink, but she seemed so elegant). I just couldn't believe my luck. She would often drink a little too much wine, but she reasoned that she was paying for the bottle and I wasn't drinking, so she was probably having a little more than usual. This made sense to me, and somewhere in my head, I blamed myself for her drinking a little too much.

I told her all about my life—my childhood and addiction, my dad's cruelty and my love for him in spite of it. When I told her about my father being killed by my brother, she held me and I cried. I cried good, therapeutic, cleansing tears, and she made it seem OK. I had never cried in front of anyone, and this bonded us in some weird way. It was new territory for me. I had slept with many women, but this was a level of intimacy that was new. It was scary, but Melissa knew the right words or when to be quiet. She taught me a man can cry and still be a man. Everything felt right with her, I was overwhelmed with gratitude to God for allowing me the company of one of His angels. Life would be perfect from now on.

Melissa wouldn't have sex with me. She was a good girl, and good girls make guys wait. I was patient—unhappy about the lack of sex, but willing to wait for her to say OK. We kissed with great passion, though. She felt wonderful in my arms, and I was going crazy with desire for her. Three weeks had passed and still no sex. We spent every waking hour together. If she wasn't at work, she was by my side. She would drop me off at 9:00 every night because that was curfew at Nehemiah House on weekdays, but as soon as I figured she was home, we were on the phone talking about the next day's plans or the weekend. I noticed that sometimes she sounded strange, like she wasn't quite herself, but she would just say she was tired or that the wine from dinner really hit her hard. I didn't give it another thought. After all, good girls don't lie!

She brought me home one Thursday evening, and I waited about an hour before calling her. She sounded like a totally different person on this night, and I asked her if she was alright. She said she was fine, but her words were slurred, and then I heard a male voice in the background say, "Tell him I'm here."

My world went speeding out of control, my throat went dry and my knees went weak as my mind raced at a million miles per hour. Was my angel cheating on me? Well, we weren't boyfriend and girlfriend, but I thought... My mind jumped gears. "Melissa, who's there?" It was all I could manage. She assured me she could explain and blah blah blah, but I didn't hear her words. I heard Charlie Brown's parents—words were being said, but nothing was making sense. I hung up the phone and spent a sleepless night just running over the scenarios in my head. I was furious and hurt. To put it simply, I was a mess!

The next morning I knew she was at work, so I got in the shower and then got dressed. I had about forty dollars saved up from my little survey hustle I did while Melissa was at work. I was saving up to get her something nice, so I didn't spend money on anything that I didn't have too. This morning I was taking that forty bucks and going to Greektown to get some of those black bags of dope that were around right before I got clean. Fuck it. The good life was a joke anyway. There were no good girls. In fact, all women were whores, and my mother only took the day off to give birth to me! That's how my brain was working. I was just waiting for the nine o'clock hour to hit because that's when I could sign out to go to "work." So at five of nine, I started for the office upstairs to sign out. There were a few guys hanging about who spoke when I walked in. I just muttered hellos as I signed the book. I felt like they knew I was going to get high. I hadn't done it yet, but guilt was setting in already.

As I walked downstairs a war raged inside me. I wanted the dope so I could not feel this pain. I had never faced life; I always hid behind the drugs. The only time I dealt with things in the natural was in prison, and there I could respond with vicious violence. I didn't have to work through a problem. I could just beat it, kick it, stab it, but now I was in new territory. My feelings were hurt, and I just wanted to numb it. I've always walked with my head down, but on this day I was looking at the ground along the driveway so as not to make eye contact with anyone. I didn't want to talk about it or pray about it—I wanted to go get a few caps of smack and dance with "the girl with golden eyes." I looked up and at the end of the driveway was Melissa's silver 300zx. Man, this chick had some nerve, but she didn't know how ignorant and cold I could be. At this point, she hadn't even heard me curse, but man, that was about to change!

Chapter 29
Once Bitten, Twice Shy

I walked up to the car the driver's side facing me. "What the fuck are you doing here?" I asked quickly, my tone shocking her. I could see it in her eyes. I was happy to have shocked her. I wanted her to know how angry I was.

"Get in the car. I'll take you to breakfast and explain everything." Her statement infuriated me.

"I know you pay for most things when we go out, but if you think you can fuck someone and buy me back with an Egg McMuffin, you're mistaken." I spit the words, but she smiled, just enough to make me think about the silliness of my statement and disarm me enough to walk around to the passenger's side of her car. As I rounded the car, I noticed the whole passenger side was smashed in. I opened the door with lots of effort and noise. "When did you wreck?"

She told me a grand story of how her ex-boyfriend had showed up at her house with beer and whiskey. He was already drunk and said he wanted to talk to her. Afraid he would cause a big scene, she let him in, where, after a few minutes of drunken rambling, I called and this lit the fuse. He threw beer at her and called her all kinds of names. He then went outside after her neighbor came to the door to check on her, jumped in his truck and rammed her car, doing minimal damage to his truck but really destroying the passenger's side of her car. I believed every word and why wouldn't I? Here was the evidence right in front of me. As we got to her place, I saw beer cans thrown all over the place, and I did question, at least internally, why she hadn't cleaned them up. But I quickly wrote it off. I mean I guess she wanted me to see what had happened. I made the assumption he was in jail now and told her to get a restraining order. Her next words hit me like a thunderbolt.

"Well, I don't want to get him in trouble." The words bounced around in my head and my warning bells started ringing.

"What? Fuck him!" My words were out before I thought about them. Somewhere in my subconscious I noted the ashtray overflowing with smoked cigarettes, but didn't let it enter my conscious mind. If I had, I would have said it looked more like a drunken party that got out of hand than him just showing up and starting trouble. I looked at her and saw tears welling in her eyes and I melted. Any doubts I had dissolved in those pretty blue eyes so full of hurt. What a fool I was. I held her for a moment, and she started making phone calls to the insurance company as I began cleaning up. It wasn't long before she had a rental car and hers was towed to be repaired. Underneath my calm, collected demeanor I was seething. I wanted to rip this guy limb from limb. How could he cause this beautiful little woman to cry? In that moment, I hated him, and I didn't even know his name.

Looking back, I should have seen what was right in front of me, but I was blinded by her and my own desires for the perfect little life. She knew I had questions forming and knew just what to do. The next day was Friday. She picked me up on her way home from work. We went back to her apartment that I had cleaned yesterday, and it was a lovely place. She went to the shower as I laid on the couch watching TV. She came out of the shower with a robe closed up to her neck. I was starting to think I was never going to see her naked. We started to kiss, and she halted things again. "I better go get dressed before this goes too far." I lay back on the couch and questioned how long she was gonna keep me waiting, when she said, "OK, I'm dressed. How does this look?"

She dropped her robe to reveal a black and red teddy complete with garter belt and stockings. Yes, this woman knew how to stop the nagging questions in my mind. We made love for hours. I must admit it was glorious. It had been so long since sex meant something, and so long since I had feelings for anyone. We moved together in perfect unison, a crescendo headed toward nirvana. Then, for the first time in my life, fireworks and the orchestra played in my head. This was making love! This was what I'd been looking for in so many others. To say I was happy is an understatement of epic proportions!

The relationship with Melissa progressed fast, and my relationship with God took a backseat. Before long, we were living together. I found work at a construction company making terrible money, but Melissa made decent money, so we did well. I was living the dream. I wouldn't let the glaring problems on the horizon interfere with my vision of perfection. She came home often and didn't kiss me, or when she did, I caught the odor of whiskey on her breath. She would disappear into the bedroom and when I'd look for her, she would be passed out in her work clothes. I saw that she drank too much and, on occasion, I would say yes when she asked if I wanted her to stop by the liquor store on her way home. I knew her job was demanding, and she was still my perfect little angel!

I was about four months off of heroin. I wasn't going to meetings or church. I was counting on love to keep me clean. It was payday, and we were working in the city, all day long. I was watching people go in this alley and cop drugs. My anxiety was through the roof when the boss handed me my check, I swear I planned to go straight home, but his next words sealed my relapse. "Hey, Freddie, that little bar cashes checks." He had no idea what he had said. He was just being helpful, but in minutes, I had cashed my check and copped four capsules of heroin, a brand new syringe and was on my way home, I had an hour before Melissa got off, so I raced in the house and injected a capsule of heroin. I forgot that I had to be careful because a clean junkie dies fast! We try to ingest the same amount we used to and usually check out! Janis Joplin and Jimi Hendrix come to mind. Luckily for me, I knew I had to not show any signs of being high when she came in. I cleaned up and hid my stuff, jumped in the shower, and when she called and asked if I wanted her to stop at the liquor store, I quickly said yes, thinking I could blame the booze for my condition.

She came through the door with a big smile, and I mixed us two Captain Morgans and Coke. She was in a bubbly mood and didn't have booze on her breath. She said, "I'm going to jump in the shower, but we gotta talk when I get out." Damn it, she knew I was high, but how? I was keeping my distance. Maybe she doesn't know I'm high. I thought about all the things I would say when she got out of the shower, how I'd beg her forgiveness and promise to never slip again. I had my speech all worked out. As she came out of the shower and sat on the couch next to me, I quickly realized I hadn't planned for the next words out of her mouth: "Freddie, I'm pregnant."

## Chapter 30
## Back in the Saddle

    I was stunned by her words but happy as a man can be. I sat with my mouth open, and she smiled knowing I was over the moon with joy! We kissed cried, laughed and talked about the future. We made plans. It was a wonderful beautiful moment, and she didn't notice I was higher than Fat Charles' ass at the time. I questioned her drinking, and she said she was just celebrating tonight, and that alcohol was off limits after tonight. So with that said, I agreed in my own head. I would do my last three capsules of dope over that weekend and "celebrate," then it was off limits from then on! I had a great feeling in my heart. I called my sister and told her about it. She was happy to hear I was doing so well and wanted to be part of my baby's life. My mother was still unhappy with me over the whole deal with the house, but congratulated me and even invited us to her new apartment. Life was going my way. I had met the perfect girl, she was having my baby, and I was clean (mostly). I was back in the saddle and the range looked glorious!

    The next five months I was on my best behavior. Even going to the doctors with Melissa was great! I can remember the first time I heard my son's heartbeat; tears welled in my eyes and I felt a surge of joy that no drug could touch. I really wanted to stay clean for this baby, but the truth is, I didn't understand addiction and wasn't educating myself. Trying to stay clean for someone else is the equivalent of trying not to have cancer or any other disease. I've heard it said, "If you loved me, you wouldn't use drugs!" That's like telling a cancer patient "IF you really cared about this family, you wouldn't be sick." Some people have a hard time accepting that addiction is a disease, but the research has been done and it is recognized in the medical community as a disease. I can tell you it's not a lack of love or willpower—it's a raging compulsion that lives inside us addicts.

Melissa was nearly six months pregnant. I had noticed her avoiding me after work and all that, but chalked it up to pregnancy moodiness. I thought I smelled alcohol on her a few times, but didn't accuse her of drinking, partly because I didn't want to upset her while pregnant. The other reason—and the hardest one to live with—was I didn't want to destroy my vision of perfection. I wanted to believe we were the perfect little family; I wanted to be the family on the cover of a magazine. Maybe if I had called her on her drinking, things would have been different.

It was a Thursday, I think. I had gone to work in downtown Baltimore. At the end of the day, we received our checks and I did what I had been thinking of since we started the city job. I told the guys I was going up to Charles Street to meet my girl. There were grains of truth to my story. My girlfriend did work for a law firm on Charles Street, but that's where the truths ended. I called her from the little check cashing place, and she told me she was working late. When she came home, she would be tired so she'd probably go right to bed. So I'd have to grab my own dinner and such. My plan was coming along beautifully, but little did I know she had a plan of her own. Her plan was to get outta work a little early, do some drinking with her girlfriend that wouldn't judge her, and then come in and go to bed while I dozed on the couch. My plan was to get some smack and get good and high, and when she came in, it would just look like I was dozing on the couch. We were both addicts living a lie, and the truth would soon slap us right in our lying faces!

I got my dope and went home. I missed the ritual of going to cop, getting the best smack on the street, and watching for the cops. That's part of the drug lifestyle that becomes addicting, too. Then every junkie has their own ritual for how they get high. Some hurry up and slam the drug into their vein just to get it in them, but me, I liked the setup as much as the payoff. I would lay it all out. I'd get a small cup of water, a nice deep spoon bent to lay flat, a small piece of clean cotton and a lighter. I'd put a capsule and a half of Baltimore dope called "scramble" into the spoon, then add about sixty to seventy units of water. I'd watch the fire under the spoon cook away the cut and leave a clear-to-tannish liquid, then I'd add my cocaine, just half to three-quarters of a five dollar vial. I didn't want to overpower my dope; I just wanted the coke rush, followed by the warm blanket of the heroin, enveloping me in its narcotic embrace.

After finishing up, I cleaned up and put two caps of heroin and a few nickels of coke in my little stash spot. I went to the couch, but would return to the bathroom to double check and triple check that I left no signs of drug use. Melissa came in around 8:00 p.m. and rolled right in the bedroom, for which I was grateful because I had gotten really powerful smack and was nodding in and out. However, she was at the point of drunk where they think no one can tell that they'd been drinking. So she came out and sat on the couch reeking of alcohol. I tried pulling my shit together, but she noticed. She said nothing at first, but I knew it was coming, so I started formulating a story to feed her. However, she saw it as an opportunity to get some more drinking. in. "You're high," she blurted after about ten minutes of silence.

"I am," I admitted. Then the war began, a war that would rage until the day we broke up!

Looking back, I should have gotten help early on, I was ignorant to the power of addiction, and it cost me dearly. As we argued, I told her I knew she was drinking and that it was her fault I got high. She, in turn, blamed me for her drinking. That night she did something I never could forgive and it destroyed my visions of perfection. She stood up and walked to the bedroom. I heard her rummaging around in there. After a moment, she returned with a pint of Captain Morgan Spiced Rum that was three quarters of the way full. As she brought the bottle to her lips, revulsion raged in me and love crossed the line to a hatred even I didn't understand. She guzzled the brown liquid down as I looked at her pregnant stomach. I really couldn't believe my eyes. It's hard to describe all the things I felt at that moment: revulsion, hate, fear, and maybe even pity. She drained the bottle and glared at me, then turned her back and went to the bedroom where she laid across the bed and passed out.

## Chapter 31
## You're No Good

I sat on the couch, my mind racing in a million different directions. The narcotic warmth no longer held me in its embrace, I was stone sober! How could she? How could she down a bottle of rum while sitting there pregnant? These were the words that kept ringing in my ears, but no answer came. I sat there for a long time blaming myself. I caused this by getting high again. I went to the bathroom and threw my drugs down the toilet. I cursed myself because as soon as I did it I wanted them back! I wanted my old friends to help me through another one of life's hurdles. I had always faced pain and fear the same way—by getting stoned. The drugs were gone, flushed in a moment of self-hatred. As I blamed myself, I had to admit some truths: first, ,she started drinking after work before she even knew I had relapsed; and second, it's a seasoned veteran who can drain three quarters of a pint in one pull. These truths were tearing the foundation from under my visions of perfection.

The morning came, but answers didn't! I left for work with a heart full of lead. I didn't wake her before I left. I wrote about five notes, but they all sounded empty to me, so I tore them up and threw them in the trash. When I got to the job site I found out we wouldn't be working that morning for whatever reason. As I headed for the bus stop, I saw the guy I had bought my heroin from the day before. H asked if I wanted anything. I lied and said no. I really wanted to get high, but even more than that, I wanted the perfect little life I had just 24 short hours ago. A certain part of me knew I could never get that back, but I guess sometimes the heart wants something soooooo bad it won't consider glaring facts! As I boarded the bus, my pager went off. It was Melissa. I couldn't answer since I was on the bus, but as I got off the bus I got a 911 page from Melissa. I casually walked over to a pay phone and dropped a quarter in not believing there was an emergency at home. Still, I'd play my part. She picked up and I asked, "Is everything OK?" She said it was, but sent the 911 because she thought I was avoiding her. "So I guess you hate me now, huh?" she asked.

"I don't hate you, Melissa. I'm stunned by your actions, but I don't hate you!" She did what she was a master at—turning it all around on me, and within a few minutes, I was apologizing to her. I was wrong for using again, but these were separate issues she blended together. What I didn't know at the time was that Melissa was a professional victim. She took no responsibility for herself; she just blamed others. I had no idea what I was in store for with this girl, but things were about to go bad and continually get worse.

I walked through the door. She was laying on the couch after having cleaned up the apartment and herself. She appeared to be in pain, and I asked what was wrong. "Oh, I didn't want to upset you on the phone, but I've been having pains this morning." Alarms were going off, but within an hour they had passed and everything was cool. I relaxed and looked forward to the weekend off. I went to the video store and got some movies, and on the way home, bought some chicken wings. Friday night we laid around watching movies and relaxing. At around 11:00 p.m. she started talking about this pizza shop on Belair Road. I knew she was craving pizza and jumped in her car and got the guy to stay open fifteen minutes late to make my pregnant girlfriend her favorite pizza. It was a really nice night, and I remember it so well because it was to be the last nice night for a long time to come.

In the morning, I awoke to this screaming bird that had a nest in the tree right next to my bedroom window. I'm no bird expert, so I don't know what kind it was, but I'll tell you this— he's lucky there wasn't a gun in the house. Melissa awoke and ran to the bathroom, and I went in and held her hair back as she got violently ill. I blotted her face with a cold rag and got her back to bed. I told her to call the doctor while I got her some medicine for her stomach. I went to the pharmacy and spent close to sixty dollars on over-the-counter medicine. When I returned home, she said the doctor told her to come to the hospital. I was a little upset. I mean, she was only six months pregnant so there was no way the baby was coming yet! I grabbed the bag we kept by the door anyway, figuring it would be a good drill for when the time "really" came. I hustled her to the car and drove her to the hospital. We got inside and they took her straight back, I went to park the car and had a smoke, confident I would be taking her back home in an hour or so.

I walked back inside the hospital and the people were so nice. They showed me to her room. As I pulled back the sheet, I was shocked to find five people around Melissa. What I didn't know was she was in labor!! They were giving her this medicine and said they would check back in an hour. The group made its exodus, leaving Melissa and me with our mouths hanging open. "What's going on, baby? You're in labor? How can that be?" She had no answers, only more questions, and fear was jumping up and down on my shoulder whispering all the terrible things that could happen if they couldn't stop the labor. I was trying to piece things together, but in that moment, I simply couldn't think straight.

A very nice nurse came in and checked Melissa to see if she had dilated anymore. She was very talkative and trying to put our fears to rest, but she was talking about premature babies and her words hit like a tsunami to my soul. "We don't know what causes these things. Sometimes babies are just ready to come out. Other times it's from poor dieting by the mother , smoking, or the biggest no-no there is, drinking alcohol while pregnant."

She kept talking, but I didn't hear another word for what seemed like an eternity. I pictured Melissa putting that bottle up to her lips. The thought turned my stomach, and Melissa knew exactly what was going through my mind and said, "No, I didn't do any of those things." I just stared at her. In that moment, I hated her more than anything I've ever hated.

The next words I heard were the nurse's. "One thing's for certain—this baby is coming, and it's coming today!"

Chapter 32
Ain't Life Grand

As far as labor goes, I suppose this was one of the fastest. It seemed to me the nurse said "This baby is coming today!" and the next minute, he was here. I knew immediately that something was wrong. The baby came out, and I heard the doctor and nurses whispering to one another. But I also heard my son let out a scream, so I knew he was breathing. They swaddled him up and hustled him over to the warmer. They wouldn't let me get close, and I was getting angry, but they assured me they wanted to get his weight and such first, then I could see him. The doctor sent most of the nurses away and then he delivered news that would cause me to hate Melissa beyond words.

"Your son is four pounds two ounces, but he has well developed lungs, so we are sure we can get his weight up. However," the doctor continued, "he was born with a cleft lip and a cleft palate. He's going to have to be in N.I.C.U. for at least thirty days." I was stunned. I didn't know what a cleft lip or a cleft palate was, but I certainly knew it was bad enough to keep him in intensive care for thirty days, and I was seething inside. I looked at Melissa and anything I thought I still felt for her vanished. I wanted to grab her by the shoulders and say look at what you've done, you drunkin' bitch! But I didn't say anything. I simply left the room and went outside to smoke a cigarette. As I smoked, I made a decision. I was going to go through this with her, but as soon as the baby came home, I was leaving her, getting a lawyer and taking my son away.

Friends and family poured into the hospital. I didn't want to see them, but I knew there was no way to stop it either. One of my old so-called friends came in with his girlfriend. The girlfriend was stoned and nodding in and out. I wanted to get high so bad, and here she was, smacked out of her mind. I walked out of the room and went to the bathroom. When I came out of the stall, my so-called friend was still there, and boy, was he reading me wrong. "Fred, don't be embarrassed by this. It's nobody's fault." I wasn't embarrassed, and yes, it was someone's fault, but I just kinda mumbled an answer. As I turned from the sink he opened his palm and had four capsules of heroin in it. I looked at the dope. I wanted it so bad. I hated Melissa and I hated the guy standing in front of me, but my most serious, burning hatred was reserved for one person: me. I reached out and took two capsules of smack.

He handed me a syringe, and I went back in the stall to seal my fate. As the heroin raced through my veins, I knew I was in trouble. I missed the warm embrace so bad, and the heroin brought on the same peace felt the day my brother injected me with Dilaudid when I was just a kid. I wasn't worried, I wasn't angry—I was wrapped in the warm blanket that is heroin's calling card. It's only after you're completely strung out that the cold, frozen hands of death replace that warmth. Melissa and I would be together for another year and a half, but the truth is, we broke up that day when she destroyed my visions of perfection. I returned to my first love, the girl with golden eyes who usually speaks in Persian—sweet sister heroin.

I spent the next thirty days in a cycle of hospital, work,

home for a quick shower, then back to one or the other. Most days I would leave work, go home and get a shower, go to the hospital and stay until morning, then go straight back to work. There were many days where I was an hour or two late because I was using more and more often. By the time the baby came home from the hospital, I was strung out again. It was self-pity, self-loathing and a number of other things that led me back to the drug, but without treatment, it was inevitable that I would end up using again. Contrary to what some say, there is no cure for addiction. It isn't a matter of willpower, and love won't keep you sober. The disease lives inside me, and it's only through a belief in a higher power, the adoption of a step program and a daily dose of those things that my disease becomes manageable.

The baby came home with special feeding bottles and countless doctor's appointments, along with many different instructions from friends, family and coworkers, who all had a friend who knew a guy that parked cars for the parent of a child with a cleft lip and palate. One day Melissa's mother showed up, a reformed coke queen from the '70s. She wanted our son the moment she saw him, and we played right into her hands.

I won't take you through all the details, but I'll give you a quick rundown of our descent into the abyss of addiction. My life, now that I returned to drugs, hit the skids very fast. I came in one night an hour late from work. I wasn't trying to hide my drug use anymore, and she wasn't hiding her drinking, at least not from me. She had made it known to everybody that I was a drug user, but she kept her own addiction under wraps.

On this particular night I came in from work, I went straight to the bathroom where I did two capsules of heroin. I took my shower and got dressed. As I came into the living room, she was waiting on me. "I want some of your dope!"

She had caught me off-guard. She was a juicer, and on this night, she was sober and asking me for heroin.

"Melissa, this stuff is no joke. You should stick to your whiskey."

She looked at me and spoke as if I hadn't said a word. "I know where you get it, and if I wanted to, I could get my own." Her words weren't mean or combative. Her tone was conversational, but there was an ultimatum being laid down.

I looked at her in shock, but quickly gathered my thoughts. "If you want some of this, grab me a mirror and I'll give you a line to snort, but be warned—most people get sick their first time around."

Her next words were like a sledgehammer to my chest. "No mirror. I want to do it the way you do it."

I hit the roof. "There's no way I'm letting you shoot up. You have no idea what you're playing with!"

She stayed calm and said, "I can do it with you where you know I'm doing a safe amount, or I can do it with someone else." It was obvious she had been thinking about this for some time. She had figured out my reaction and her response. We were about to put the final nail in our collective coffin.

## Chapter 33
## Get Your Wings

I cooked up a little less than half a capsule and injected it into her arm. She sank back into the couch, and I watched her eyes as the heroin took effect. She was feeling incredible when a wave of nausea hit her and she ran to the bathroom. She spent most of the night in the bathroom. By 6:00 a.m., she had long ago given the contents of her stomach to the toilet bowl. She was now dry heaving. I was content in the belief that she had learned her lesson and wouldn't want to do that again anytime soon. She came out of the bathroom as I was getting ready for work. "Bet you don't want anymore."

I laughed, but my laughter died off as her next words penetrated my thoughts. "Are you kidding me? I love it!"

Melissa took to heroin like a fish takes to water. She was right at home in the oblivion the drug provides early on. Things spun out of control fast and looking back, many, many things transpired between that night and our breakup, but it's the same story you already know, so I'll give you the condensed version. We tried to maintain for awhile, only getting high on weekends, never using more than three days in a row and all the limits junkies put on ourselves. None of it lasts and it always ends the same—sooner or later you are using every day, then you're too sick to go to work so you get fired, then you sell your possessions. The baby goes to Grandma's house for the weekend when you get evicted, then that weekend turns into a court hearing where Grandma gets temporary custody because the judge sees you're thirty pounds underweight and you have a pending shoplifting charge. Then you give up and steal every day to feed an insatiable demon. You inject poison and hope to die, only to wake with a million bugs on you and a million snakes in you which is one way to describe the wretchedness of withdrawal.

When you can't steal anymore, she sneaks off and sells the one thing she has left: sex to the highest bidder, and when she comes back with dope, you act like you don't know where she's been because you want the dope. You stop kissing her on the lips and you two act like you don't hate each other, but secretly, one blames the other for the what your life has become. It's an ugly, filthy existence and Satan is howling with laughter as you slowly kill each other one needle stick at a time.

It finally ended for us when I got caught shoplifting for the umpteenth time. I ended up in jail, and she took up with some guy who would support her dope habit. I went to the county with three pending court cases. I weighed in at 150 lbs. with my eyes the color of lemons from hepatitis. Somehow I only got sentenced to fourteen months, but I asked the judge to send me to jail. He couldn't believe his ears, but I was tired of this life. I needed a break from the dope and that's just what I got: a short break. I worked out every day for fourteen months. I ate and played basketball and walked out of the prison 205 lbs. of solid muscle. I had no parole because I did my time in full, so I moved to Delaware. My older sister would give me a place to stay, and I didn't know any dope dealers—or anyone else for that matter.

It does an addict little good to move to a new town. Unless that town is in Siberia, the junkie will find dope or some form of opiate. I had fallen into this pattern of getting strung out, then going to jail and kicking the habit, getting strong only to come home to do it all over again. This time would be no different, with one exception. The Bible says that when a demon gets exorcised it will come back to the host after a period of time, and when the demon sees a nice clean soul to corrupt, he brings back seven more demons with him. I can attest to that because each time I came home nice and clean, the addiction got stronger and stronger. I would find myself taking bigger chances until it just became a way of life for me. It's sad and pathetic, but it's amazing what a person will accept as normal. Ask the battered woman why she stays with her abuser. Many will say, "I just thought this was life." Being an addict is not living, it's existing. My existence was becoming more shallow and depraved, but it was all I knew. I didn't know about recovery or anything like it. I had heard of methadone, but I thought that was worse than heroin. And even though I saw people doing well on the methadone program, it wasn't for me.

Moving to Delaware should have been a good thing, and in many ways it was, but moving twenty minutes from Philly for an addict is a sure trip back into hell. I was about to enter one of the most violent phases of my life. I would participate in things that give me nightmares to this day. The next ten years of my addiction would be the absolute lowest points in my life, and I'm about to share some of them. The names have been changed to protect the not-so-innocent.

## Chapter 34
Freak on a Leash

I made some good moves when I came to the little state I now love. I found work, got a nice truck and met a pretty girl. I also made connections I shouldn't have, but the worst was a guy I'll call George. He was an ex-cop with a sadistic streak a mile wide. Our common ground was, you guessed it, heroin. We met through mutual friends and started going to Philly together on the weekends. I was working at a refinery, and he was a correctional officer of all things. We would go cop dope, get high and go to the strip clubs in Philly. I was at home in Philly and around strippers.

I was back in my pattern. The job was first to go, and of course, the money ran low. Now I had a habit, and I was in the same fix I've been in many times. However, like I said, it gets worse each time, and it happened very fast. I woke up and rolled out of bed, the monkey already jumping up and down on my shoulder, I had no money and was in need of a fix in the worst way. I called George. "Hey, man, you have any money today?" I asked, getting straight to the point.

"Come pick me up at that church by my house. I got a way to get us a few bundles." I was already on the way before he hung up the phone. He said a few bundles, and that meant I was going to get good and high today! I knew the church he was talking about, I had picked him up there a few times. He did part-time work there and the preacher always paid him in cash, so I thought nothing of it when I pulled in the parking lot and he came running out. "Pull around back and open the tailgate." That didn't sound unnatural. I figured he was loading his tools up. He walked out with some canvass bags. He quickly loaded them in the bed of the truck and jumped in.

"Let's go," he quipped as I shifted into gear.

"Man, that don't look like tools. Please tell me we're not stealing from a church," I said, half joking, unsure what was in the bags.

"Look, bro, do you wanna get high"?

I didn't answer. I didn't have to. He knew I wanted to get high and even though I was balking at the idea, he knew I'd go through with it. He knew I was troubled by it and tried to lighten the mood. "Go home later, say three Our Fathers and seven Hail Mary's and I'll absolve you, my son." He laughed, but I didn't. We pulled into a place where we had sold stolen items in the past. I sat in the car while he went inside to sell the items, which is unheard of for two junkies. One never trusts the other to tell him the truth about how much he got for the items. However, I wanted to distance myself from this act. I knew stealing from a church would bring bad things, and it did.

We got high that day but the next few days everything we did or tried just fell through or went wrong. It was about a week after the church deal. I picked up George up, and we headed for Philly. He had some coins to sell. Once we got there, we ended up getting 20 dollars for the coins, and I was furious. We saw a guy George knew and he started talking to the guy, trying to get him to give us six bags till later. The guy pulled the dope out of his sock, then put it back. He was talking like he was gonna do it, but then would run over to a passing car to make a sale and the talking would resume. I was sitting in the car with the illness of withdrawal making me crazy. I took as much as I could, and then I don't know what came over me. Before I knew what I was going to do, I jumped out of the car, stepped around George and hit this guy with a right hook that knocked him unconscious before he hit the ground. Fury took over and I started beating on this guy while George looked on stunned. The whole time I'm beating on the dope dealer, I'm screaming at him, "You couldn't just shut your big fuckin' mouth and give him the dope, could you?" The guy was unconscious, so don't ask me who I was talking to, but my arms got tired, so I started kicking the guy. It was ugly, and George finally pulled me off him and got me in the car. George took his dope and money and jumped in the driver's side.

We got a few miles away when I grabbed the dope George had put in the console. I cooked up five bags and shot up while he was still driving. George didn't know I was like that. I was always calming him down or being the voice of reason, so he didn't know what to make of me now. "Damn, boy, that's some right hook you got there!"

I just looked at him. The heroin had brought me back down to my mellow self. I could never explain the rage that lived inside me. Little did I know it then, but George's mind was at work formulating a plan. We split the money and dope and went our separate ways. I went home and got in the shower, ate and went to bed. I wasn't crazy about violence, but I had always lived with it and accepted it as a necessary tool.

The next day I still had dope, but I was going to run to Philly to cop some more with the money we stole. I called George and asked him if he wanted to go, and of course, he did. When I picked up George, he was as giddy as a schoolgirl. "Hey, slugger," he said, getting in my truck. I just smiled. I always knew that if it came down to it, I'd beat George's ass, but now he knew it, too. George could fight, but he was a wild man who liked to hurt people. I usually thought about what I was doing and used violence only when I deemed it necessary. Unfortunately, there were times when I lost control. He told me he wanted me to come back to his house after we got our dope. I figured he had stolen something and wanted to brag on it.

Buying dope in Philly is a strictly business operation. You pull up to a corner and however organized they are dictates what happens next. Highly organized corners will have lookouts posted for police, enforcers watching to make sure the stick-up boys don't try anything and a runner to come get your money, who then signals another guy to bring you your dope. The money and drugs stay separate at all times. Less organized corners will have fewer lookouts and no enforcers. The guy walks up and takes your money and hands you the dope. It doesn't take long for addicts or police to figure out which corners have their acts together and which corners were asking for a pinch (arrest). George and I knew a lot of corners, and the different procedure at each one. After copping our dope, we headed back to his house, went in his garage and got high. That's when I asked him what he had to show me.

He was smiling from ear to ear when he pulled open a drawer. It had a couple guns, some badges and bulletproof vests. "Brother, I seen your moves yesterday. We are gonna get paid." He laughed as he spoke the words. He was thinking about money and drugs, but I was thinking about someone getting killed and someone getting life and neither of those things appealed to me.

## Chapter 35
## Balls to the Wall

"Man, we can sell this shit and stay high for a week," I said, pulling the Kevlar out, but George had different thoughts.

"Or we can use this shit and keep the dope rolling in," he quickly added. I looked at his inventory. He had two guns—one a nice Glock that most cops carry, but the other was a rusted .38, the exact model my father had been murdered with.

"Look at this gun, George. It's rusted. Does it even fire?"

"Oh, it fires, and after I clean it up it'll be fine. But you can carry the Glock if it makes you feel better."

George wanted to take down corners. The idea was that two white guys in a late-model car with guns and vests would be accepted as cops anyway, so let's play the part. George was an ex-police officer. He showed me many things about how to handle a gun and how to present myself in a manner that would be accepted as a cop. I was unsure, and he knew it, so he played to my vanity, "C'mon, man, you know more about police procedure then some cops. You definitely been in the game longer than most of those rookies with a badge. You're smart, man, and you know the streets. You're the only person I trust to do this with! Why do you think this stuff has been in my garage just rusting away? Look, brother, I have the perfect corner in the Badlands. There's two, three guys tops. We hit them fast and hard, and by the time they figure out we ain't cops, we will be long gone."

I had dope and money on me, so I was in no hurry to run up on these corners. I told George I'd think about it, but a huge smile broke out on his face when I said, "Clean that rusted thing up while I'm thinking!" The truth is, I had thought about it for a long time and knew I was going to as soon as George showed me the tools of the trade. The rest of the week I got high from the strong-arm score and cruised the streets of Philly. George showed me the corner that he said would be a fast couple grand, and it did look easy, but I knew in the back of my mind that any easy score can turn into a twenty-year bit in a moment. George had vast knowledge from his former time as a cop and from his current job as a correctional officer. A pack of Newport would end up getting one of our biggest scores, but more on that in a bit.

The day came that we were ready to hit that easy corner in the Badlands, a notorious part of Philadelphia, but an unorganized crew for sure. I was nervous as hell while driving to pick up George. He came out with two duffel bags and threw them in the trunk of my girlfriend's car, and we headed for Philly, neither of us talking for the first part of the ride. But as we got closer, George started going over the drill we had practiced fifty times, and I knew he was talking because he was nervous, but I just wanted to do it and be done with it. We pulled into the Badlands and rode past the corner. It was a warm spring day and business was steady, so we went to the bottom of the block and George got out his high powered binoculars. He then said the words that would become our war cry. "Suit up. We go in two."

It was crazy. I watched George become a militarized machine, all business as we put on the vest and baseball hats that said POLICE in bold yellow letters. I put the holstered Glock on my hip, and I have to say I felt like a cop.

It may seem strange, but once you step into the role, it comes very natural. Instead of saying "Yes" it's "Affirmative." I guess after years of being around cops, the lingo becomes ingrained. As we headed toward the corner, my heart was beating out of my chest. I was afraid I would drop the gun or do something very stupid, but as we pulled up, a calm took over and while my adrenaline was wide open, I became a cop for the next 45 seconds. We rolled to a stop and were out of the car before anyone noticed us, "Police! Get your hands where I can see them!" I yelled in my most authoritative tone. The kid looked up, caught completely off-guard. There were three of them, and they had nowhere to go, with me on one side, George on the other, and a brick wall behind them.

"Turn around and put your hands on the wall!" George barked at them. "You got 'em, partner. And if one of them so much as blinks, they will die in the dark." I stole a line from some movie, but it worked. They stayed stock still as George took money and dope off of all three. While we were watching them earlier, they would run over to this burned-out car, so we knew that's where they kept whatever stash they had.

"Cuff them while I run their names," George said as he walked over to the burned-out car and grabbed a McDonald's bag out of it. I only had one set of cuffs and didn't know what to do.

"Just keep your hands on the wall," I instructed the dazed trio. I turned to look over my shoulder. George was in the car, so I quickly holstered my gun and made it to the car. We were around the corner and gone before they even thought we might not be cops. We jumped on 95 and were at George's house in minutes. I was so high from the robbery itself that I hadn't even shot any dope yet. We were laughing and high-fiving each other before we even took a look at our take. In a few moments, we had counted $700 in many wrinkled, dirty denominations and fifteen bundles of heroin, each bundle containing thirteen bags. It's worth noting that in Baltimore they sell capsules of heroin, but in Philadelphia, they sell little blue wax paper bags inside clear plastic that's heat sealed at each end.

"Didn't I tell you this was easy money?" George asked as we divided the money and drugs between us. "I already have the next corner picked out," he continued as he sat there still wearing the vest. I had gotten out of mine pretty quickly. I wasn't exactly comfortable in cop clothes.

"OK, man, but we gotta give it a few days. Let's not push our luck." I chided him.

"Sure, sure Freddie, no problem. Let's enjoy our take for now."

I had to admit I enjoyed the rush of the robbery, as well, but I also knew things could get really ugly, so I wanted to do the homework. George was ready to run and gun!

We got high in his garage, and George sat at his workbench nodding in and out. I wanted some distance between Philadelphia and me, so I jumped in my girlfriend's car and headed home. I thought about what we did and where it could lead. I told myself I'd only do robberies when I had nothing else going on. It's amazing how often it turned out I had nothing else going on.

## Chapter 36
## Nowhere to Run

Sticking up dope dealers became a regular thing for George and me. Pretty soon we were known around the Badlands as Starsky & Hutch, a name George was quite fond of. Our act was so good that most thought we were real cops, just dirty, though sine knew we were just robbers and beefed up security. We were taking in lots of money and drugs, but the only thing that happens then is your habit gets bigger and bigger. We were pushing our luck and I knew it. George seemed oblivious and was getting more reckless. Soon we would be nose to nose ready to fight. I'd be lying if I said I didn't see it coming.

It started out as a regular day. We were in Philly, watching a corner on 2nd and Cambria in an ugly part of the city. I had dope and money and wasn't really ready to "work," but George wanted to hit this particular corner because they kept dope, coke and weed right there in a stash house. It was a three-man team with a woman watching the stash. I agreed it was a quick grab and could be a nice score. We had paid a prostitute for the info and she and George were communicating this morning. The main man was supposed to deliver a big package in the next half hour. George was watching the corner through binoculars. We were sitting in a rented car because we couldn't use my girlfriend's car anymore. As soon as I pulled on the block in her car, kids would start yelling, "One time, Starsky &Hutch!!!" alerting everyone the "police" were around.

I could tell by George's body language that the package was being delivered. He kept watching, and then said the words I'd heard so many times before "Suit up!" We had upgraded our equipment. We had bulletproof vests, baseball hats and windbreakers, all with "POLICE" written across them in bold letters. We both had Glocks now and badges that hung around our necks. George was short and stocky with a bald head. Even without the gear he had cop written all over him. Me, not so much. I had long dark hair and multiple tattoos, muscular from many prison sentences and looked more at home in a biker bar. However, many undercover cops cultivate the biker look to infiltrate drug circles, so I still passed, especially with all the official looking gear.

We rolled up on the corner, my adrenaline flowing. In seconds, we were out of the car, but George deviated from the plan and went straight for the stash house. We were supposed to get the three guys secure, then hit the house together. As a result, two of the dealers got away. I caught one guy and put him on the hood of my car. I was going through the regular motions, but George was taking forever. "Where's your ID?" I ask, just killing time, but my heart was beating out of my chest. I looked up to see a police car headed my way. I couldn't believe this! I was about to be arrested for impersonating a police officer, multiple felonies, and if they linked me to the other crimes, I was going to a prison for a very long time, surrounded by the guys I stuck up!! All these things ran through my mind in an instant as the cops rolled up to the corner.

I don't know how to explain it to the reader, but a calm

came over me. I knew there was a good chance I was going to jail, but those odds get worse when one panics. I threw up a two- finger salute and continued with my "suspect." The uniformed officer in the passenger's side leaned out the window. "You need us?"

"Nah, we're good," I said with my best Philly Italian inflection. He saluted, and they rolled past. I left my "suspect" standing there and ran in the house. "George, where the fuck are you? We gotta go, and I mean now!"

I rounded the corner to find George over top of this terrified Puerto Rican girl bending four of her fingers back as she screamed out, "It's in the closet, under the floorboards. Please stop hurting me!"

I looked at George with total disgust as he headed to the closet still talking to the girl. "You better not be lying, you bean-eating bitch, or I'll break the rest of your fingers." George grabbed two duffel bags out of the floorboards and an AK-47 that was in there, as well. I was already out the door and headed for the car.

I couldn't believe it, but my "suspect" was still standing where I left him. A small crowd had gathered. I quickly uncuffed him as George threw the bags and weapon in the backseat. In ten minutes, we were headed south on 95. George was ecstatic over the assault rifle, but I was shook by a few things, and at this point, George still didn't know how close we came to being locked up. As we drove toward his house, he was doing all the talking, but I really wasn't listening. I kept picturing the girl from the stash house with the big tears rolling down her face and the mangled hand she had thanks to us, and my God, what was the big dealer going to do to her for losing his stash! I was being bombarded with remorse!

We pulled into George's yard and brought the two bags and the rifle into the garage. It wasn't until we were in there with the door closed that I finally spoke. "George, what the fuck is wrong with you?!"

He looked at me as if I slapped him and answered with, "What are you talking about? This is a great score."

"Why did you hurt the girl? I don't like that shit," I said, looking him dead in the eye.

"I didn't hurt her. Not really. I broke a few fingers because the stupid bitch wouldn't tell me where the stash was. What's going on, Fred? Are you going soft on me? What do you think she would have done if she got to this before I got to her?" he asked, holding up the AK-47.

"I guess we'll never know, but did you know a marked police car rolled up while you were inside? I got rid of them, but man, if they would have stopped, we would be in jail!"

"Yes, but you handled it. You did your job and I did mine. We're home, we're safe, and we have two duffel bags I'd really like to go through instead of standing here arguing over a robbery that went as planned!"

George had his own logic going, and I wasn't going to make him see my point of view, so I just let it go. Our score was bigger than anything we had ever done before. I couldn't believe all the dope and cash that was in the duffel bags as we dumped them out. I grabbed some dope and a little coke and quickly did a speedball. We split the money and drugs. I still had all the police gear on, including the Glock on my hip, as I headed for the car. I threw my half of the take into one of the duffel bags and stuck it in the wheel well. George said, "Hey, man, what do you wanna do about the rifle?"

I knew one thing for certain—I didn't want it. "You seem to like it, George. Throw me three hundred and call it even."

George couldn't get the money out fast enough. Soon I was on 95, headed home. I had money, I had drugs and I had all the things that go along with that life! So why was I so unhappy? It would later become crystal clear that God was guiding my steps, but in that moment, I felt very far from Him. I believe it was God that had me walk away from that AK-47, and I'm so grateful He did. Things were headed downhill fast!

## Chapter 37
## Happy Trails

A few days would pass before George would call me, and when I answered the phone, I never dreamed he wanted to hit a corner so soon, but he did! I couldn't believe what I was hearing. George was on the other end of the phone telling me he had no dope or money.

"George ,what the hell did you do? I'm still sitting pretty, and the other day shook me up. We almost got busted!" I was not ready to pull another stick-up. Things were getting dangerous and I had a real nice stash to ride it out with. My plan was to let things cool down for a few months. I didn't like the direction we were going, and I was sure someone was going to get seriously hurt. In truth, I wanted out altogether.

"OK, I'll tell you what happened." he began. I won't bore you with the details, but let me give you a brief description of why George was broke and hurting already. It seems he had taken the entire stash to a hotel along with two females he hardly knew. They partied and had sex till he passed out, waking only to find the girls gone, along with his drugs and money. Easy come, easy go! How stupid can one person be, but I don't suppose he was thinking at the time.

"Look, George, I'll bring you a few bundles, but I'm not hitting any corners," I said, not mentioning how stupid I thought he was for getting his stuff stolen.

"A few bundles will get me through a few hours. I need to hit a corner, and I have the perfect one, but we're going to need two extra guys."

"Are you out of your fuckin' mind?" I exploded. "George, we're headed for trouble. If you want to get killed or get thirty-five to life, then keep going, but I'm taking some time off!" George wanted to hit a corner where the crews were well-organized, well-armed and ready to throw down.

It may seem silly, but I think the AK-47 we had was making George feel invincible. We had seen this corner many times and even copped dope from there in the past. We had agreed that the corner was set up too well, and that it would be really dangerous to hit it. We believed the real cops stayed away because it was too dangerous to take down, and there were rumors they paid the cops off, but who knows? This particular place was set up at the end of the block. The block led to a dead end, so if you were in a car, there was only one way in and one way out. This drug crew had literally taken over the block. They had lookouts on the roofs armed with assault rifles and walkie-talkies. They had lookouts at street level wearing pistols in plain sight, along with enforcers on foot and in cars. They kept the dope in a different house every day so you had to watch them to see which house, and it's hard to watch someone when guys are on the roof with binoculars looking back at you. Also, this crew was known to be all business and very dangerous. Many bodies in the streets were attributed to this clique.

I hung up the phone and sat there thinking. If I hit this corner, I could probably take two months off. The extra guys George had in mind were his ex-police buddies, so they would know what they were doing. However, the bad outweighed the good, and it would be for nothing if we were killed. I did some heroin and looked at what I had on hand. I had plenty of dope and a pile of money I hadn't even counted. It would be foolish to do this job. As I sat thinking, my phone rang. I didn't want to pick it up because I knew it was George I answered after many rings and the following are the last words George and I ever spoke to each other. "Man, we have been through a lot of shit together, so I'm only going to ask you this one time. Are you in or out?"

I sat looking at the floor as I contemplated my answer. To this day I don't like ultimatums, so my word came out in a short burst "Out!" The phone went dead in my hand.

I sat there holding the phone for a long time before I placed it back on the receiver. My sister knocked at my door, and I opened it. She was standing there with orange juice and two BLT sandwiches. "Freddie, you've been down here for two days, and as far as I know, you haven't ate a thing. Take these sandwiches and please eat them." I took them without a word. My mind was still on George and the robbery. I had plenty of dope and money and I thought I was fooling everyone, but I looked bad again. I wasn't eating or getting any sun. I lived like a vampire sleeping all day and rising at night. I hated myself and what I had become. I covered the mirror on my dresser so I didn't have to catch a glimpse of me. My veins were collapsing from years of sticking myself with dull needles. I wanted to talk to someone but who could I go to? My sister wouldn't understand. She had never even smoked pot. She lived in a white-bread world. She had raised a great son who had a good job and had succeeded where I had failed. My mom was living in a decent little apartment and would call me once in awhile to heap some guilt on me and then talk about her favorite subject in the world, my older brother Steve. I felt so alone inside the prison I had made, and I was recessing further.

The rest of that night I waited for the phone call. I wanted to hear George laughing on the other end, telling me how I'd missed the greatest score ever, but that call never came. In fact, I would never see or speak to George again.

Here's what I was able to put together about that night. George got off the phone with me and had two other guys go with him. They weren't ex-cops or experienced with weapons. They were young guys who looked up to George and wanted badly to impress him. Rumor has it that the look-out boys had them made before George and his boys made it up the block. George and one guy got out of the car, but didn't make it two steps before gunfire erupted. George was shot twice, once in the leg and once in the chest. He got off a few shots with the AK-47 and killed one of the dope dealers. The guy who got out of the car with George was killed instantly, shot in the forehead. The driver panicked and took off, but they shot him a few times before he got off the block, crashing the car a few blocks away after passing out from blood loss. The driver and George lived. George was in the hospital for months before going to prison. They charged him with two murders, including his friend's, and a laundry list of crimes. George went to a prison somewhere in Pennsylvania where he was stabbed to death a few months later.

Did I feel guilty? Yes, I did! Did I feel responsible? Yes, in some ways. George and I weren't the best of friends. Our relationship was built around drugs, but you don't spend every day with someone for a year and not feel something when they get locked up or pass away. There are many things that happened over the course of my addiction, and if I put all of them in this book, it would be many volumes thick, but I've told you this story, and maybe that's my tribute to George. Recovery is an ongoing process, and I'll have to think about that for awhile. It was an event that would lead me down a very dark road—one of the darkest in my life, but I've found it's a true statement when folks say it's always darkest before dawn.

## Chapter 38
## Black Days

I don't know that I fell into despair or anything like that; I just didn't want to end up dead or in jail. I rode for a long time on the drugs and money I stole, but it ran out and I was back to square one. A place I had been many times. Broke, dope sick and nowhere to turn. A few relationships came and went , I got put out of my sister's house and lived with one girl for a bit, then another girl for a bit. I'd clean up for a month or two and then fall back into the mighty grip of drugs all over again. Jobs came and went; I got fired from some and walked off of a few. I couldn't work without dope. Life was just a mess, but I came to accept it as a simple fact that I would probably just overdose one day and didn't really care when that day was. In fact, the sooner the better, or so I thought at the time.

One employer along the way stands out. I'll call him Jimmy. I was up on a ladder putting shutters on a house, which is probably the easiest job in construction, but being dope sick was making it difficult. My boss had a small operation, but he was a straight-laced family man. He had a wife, 2.4 kids, the single home in a nice development and a minivan. If he had any addiction it was to the candy he kept in large bowls in his work truck. This guy would eat candy all day long and would go out of his way to get more. On this particular day, he was holding the ladder while I was installing shutters. I was taking way too long and he said, "Man, Freddie, what's up with you today?"

I came down the ladder. "Do you really want to know?" I asked a little more sharply than I intended.

"Well, yeah, man you look terrible. You're dropping stuff, and it's taking you thirty minutes to do a five-minute job!"

I looked at the ground out of shame and because I was sure that Mister Lilly-white would never understand. "I need some dope or I need to go home!"

He stared at me for a minute and said get in the truck. I started to protest, but I had lost jobs before, and the truth was, I wasn't any good to him or myself, so I might as well pack it in. We drove in silence for five minutes, and then his words caught me completely off-guard. "So are you gonna tell me how to get there or not?"

I was shocked. Was Mr. All-American taking me to the hood to cop heroin? It turned out he grew up in Philly and had seen drug addiction up close, and while he didn't use them himself, he never looked down on me for my drug use. It worked pretty well for awhile, but work slowed down and he went to work for a bigger company. He was very happy when he heard I cleaned up and is one of my most loyal friends to this day.

The end was nearing, but I didn't know it. I had bounced around between Maryland and Delaware. A girlfriend here, a girlfriend there. I was even married for a short period of time, but to this day, I can't remember the ceremony. I got married while on a binge of heroin, alcohol and Xanax. I put myself and those who loved me through hell during this period. I lived in a camper by a cornfield for a few months, lived in and out of motels, getting locked up here and there for shoplifting and telling tales of who I used to be, some of them true, some not. I lived on a farm at one point working for the owner. He had twenty-six acres and a framing business. I lived in a small apartment over top one of his garages. It was fine in the beginning, but when you're using drugs, it's always just a matter of time before things go bad. I had given myself over to the unpleasant truth that this was just the way life was. I would watch the "normal" people and despise them. They'd be going to work or playing with their kid, and I'd hate them because they were everything I wanted to be. They had smiles on their faces and didn't have to have on long sleeves in 90-degree weather. I knew it was my own fault, but I couldn't stop!

I would get my drugs and cry while I was injecting them. I hated the life—my life—there was no fun left in the game. I didn't get high anymore when I used the drug; I just got well. It was never-ending maintenance, and I was getting more and more depressed, slipping deeper and deeper into the abyss. I contemplated suicide and even attempted it, but I was too much a coward to take my own life. My sister and her adult son let me move back in. They were concerned that I was gonna kill myself, but were powerless to help me. They had reservations about allowing me in the house, yet loved me enough to try and reach out to me. My sister's husband had died a few years before, and now it was just Cindy and her son, Tommy, running the house. Tommy had a good job at the brewery and Cindy was a cashier part-time, having retired from her managerial job at a large department store.

They took me in and bought me some clothes and such. I can remember that at one point I was so unkempt my nephew handed me a razor. Without a word, I took the hint and shaved. Then, neither of them understanding addiction, told me to stop using drugs. Telling a heroin addict to stop using is like telling a man with ten bullet holes in him to stop bleeding. Without treatment, it simply isn't going to happen. I repaid their kindness by stealing from them. They threw me out, and I was on the streets of Wilmington with nary a friend. I'd been in this situation before, but something was different this time. It just hurt worse. The drugs weren't working and my existence was disgrace. I had sunk to the depths of addiction—again!

I hooked up with some other homeless addicts, and they told me where the soup kitchens were and which churches would give soap and shampoo. I gleaned as much info as possible. You can learn a lot by talking to the right people. Other people who shoplift to support their habit can tell you which store has lax security and what stores buy your stolen goods. It's a little network unlike any other. I had a little duffle bag that held all my earthly possessions, but carrying that bag into a store guaranteed that I would be followed by security. We would occasionally work in pairs and use this to our advantage. One of us would carry a bag and look as suspicious as possible while another cleaned out the Tylenol rack. One of the guys told me about a church where you could put your bag in a locker and not have to carry it all the time. It was at that church where I met this little guy named David. I had some money and wanted to drop my bag and get to Riverside and cop some powerful dope everyone was talking about.

David was a volunteer at the church. He was a funny-looking, little guy who wore bib overalls and had an unlit cigarette in his mouth while he ran around doing this and that. The church did community outreach, so not only did they provide lockers, but they would give bus tokens and a list of soup kitchens. They also ran a Narcotics Anonymous meeting five days a week where you could get a pretty good cup of coffee. David, with his bushy hair and perpetual cigarette, made the coffee, gave out bus tokens, assigned lockers and if anyone needed an ID they gave vouchers to pay the cost, which David also was in charge of. Needless to say, he was always busy. When I came through the door of that church, I believe God whispered in David's ear because the little bushy-haired, chubby guy in overalls and an unlit cigarette was about to change my life!

## Chapter 39
## Diamonds on the Inside

David zeroed in on me and headed straight for me. "Hey, buddy, here's a cup of coffee. Do you need a locker? I don't have time to talk right now, but stick around after the meeting. Here's your locker key!" His words came out in a rush, as he was moving past me with two guys behind him shooting questions at him. The scene was chaotic, but David handled everyone with all the skill of a politician, working the room, signing a voucher, digging tokens out of his overalls and avoiding some that weren't grateful no matter what you did for them.

I hadn't planned on staying for the meeting, but I wanted the locker and some bus tokens would be nice so I decided to stay. I half listened as I drank two more cups of coffee, wanting it to end so I could see this guy and get my dope. As if on cue, David appeared in the doorway and motioned for me to follow him. I left the meeting and followed David to what I assumed was his office. David was all business, but I sensed a sincerity in him, a gentle kindness tempered by knowledge of the streets. In other words, he was kind but he was nobody's fool, and he got strait to the point. "What's your flavor?"

I acted like I didn't understand, but we both knew I did,

so after a moment I said, "Heroin." He smiled and pulled up his sleeve to reveal tracks that had healed but the scars from years of abuse remained. "There's another way, ya know?"

"Dude, are we about to have a Jesus talk, because I don't really believe He can help me. I tried Jesus. It didn't last." I expected to shock him or at least piss him off by rejecting what he probably held so dear, but he just smiled.

"How about detox? Have you tried that?" He asked, moving the conversation away from God.

"I don't have any insurance and keeping me in a hospital for three days is only time enough to get good and sick," I said with venom in my words.

"Man, I can see you haven't been to detox in awhile. It's different now. They give you medicine to bring you down, then they get you in a drug program. You don't need insurance. Just say the word and I'll get you a bed."

David had heard all the excuses. However, I had money in my pocket, and I just wanted to get out of there and go get high. "Let me think about it," I said and David expected my response. "Sure, man, call me when you're ready," he said, handing me a card with his name and number on it. I put the card in my wallet and headed for the bus stop, just wanting to get high and get the demon off my back.

The truth was, I hadn't considered detox. I only knew the horror stories I heard in Baltimore. It was said that they would medicate you the first day with some kind of pills that helped very little, and for three days, you had to go to meeting after meeting. On the third day, they said the drugs were out of your system and you were free to go. Here's what those brilliant doctors didn't know—withdrawal begins sixteen to twenty-four hour from your last use. In thirty-two to forty-eight hours, you're in agony! Every muscle hurts, your joints scream, nausea and diarrhea are constant companions, you can't sleep you and when you yawn, your eyes water. Eating is out of the question, so you quickly get weaker and weaker. At seventy-two hours, the withdrawal is at its greatest—you are sick as a dog and willing to do whatever it takes to feel the sweet relief of the narcotic entering your bloodstream .

I went and got my dope and walked over to a nearby park to shoot up in the portable toilet. The drug got the gorilla sated for a moment, but it was time to get back to hustling up some money for my next dose. It was a constant existence. I hadn't eaten in two days. The only thing I had besides water was a water ice some guy gave me 'cause he got his wife the wrong flavor, and I was asking the girl for a cup of water at that moment. In truth, he probably felt sorry for me. At any rate, it was the closest thing to sustenance I'd had in the past two days. I was walking along when I saw this lady taking her groceries in the house. She had just lit a cigarette, and I was going to ask if she had another, but before I could, she threw the cigarette she was smoking to the ground and hurried in the house. I wasn't about to let a nearly whole cigarette go to waste. I walked over and picked it up off the ground. I stood staring at the lipstick covered filter and something happened.

I have no idea why this moment was my moment of clarity. After all I had put myself through, I don't know why I had an epiphany at that point in time. God works in wondrous ways! Tears sprang to my eyes and my heart filled with emotion, I knew in that instant I had to make some changes. It was a feeling like never before. I felt disgust for myself; I felt the pain I had caused in so many people; I could picture my mother crying over my casket; I saw Cindy praying for me and losing sleep. It was as if I was given a glimpse into the future and the past all in a single moment. There was also something very new on the peripheral of my thoughts, something foreign. Looking back, I think it was the tiniest shard of hope. Hope and I had parted ways long ago; it's not easy to explain, but it's like a man doing a life sentence—hope is the enemy. You must give yourself over to your current state because hope causes you to think out of the now. I had long considered myself a hopeless case, but in that moment I felt hope for the first time in many years.

I hurried up the street to a pay phone when I realized I didn't have any money; not even change for a phone call. Just then a guy came walking past me. He stopped and looked at me. "Hey, man, you need change for a phone call?" He looked as stunned as me. I don't know what was going on, but I'd like to believe God was working because the guy looked as if someone were whispering in his ear, I guess I'll never know, but it's what I believe.

I fished David's card from my pocket, and he answered on the first ring. "David, it's the guy you met this morning," I began.

"Hi, Fred." I couldn't believe he remembered me, but it only confirmed that something bigger was at work here. I asked if he could get me in detox, and he asked me to call him back. I didn't have change to make a second call but I agreed. As if on cue, the same guy came out of the store. He put a Tastykake, a pint of chocolate milk and a dollar in quarters on top of the pay phone and simply said, "I've been there."

## Chapter 40
### Feels Like the First Time

Things began to happen quickly, I called David back and he told me to report to detox at 7:00 a.m. the next morning. I had no idea how I would get there or where I would stay that night, but I felt good, like I had made steps in the right direction, or at least a step! I called my sister and told her I was going into detox. She was overjoyed. I had never discussed getting help with Cindy. In fact, I had resigned myself to a life of drugs and prison long ago. She said I couldn't come to the house because her son Tommy was still furious with me, but that she would put some money in the mailbox. I made my way to her house and when I opened the mailbox she came outside. She handed me a bag with cigarettes, shampoo, soap and such. She cried and kissed me. The envelope I got from the mailbox had forty dollars in it. "Get better, Freddie," she said through tears as she closed the door.

I walked to the bus stop and heard someone calling my name. I looked and saw a friend of mine I used to get high with. I ran over and jumped in his car. "Hey, Carlos, what's going on, man?" I asked.

"Not much, Freddie. Where you headed?"

If I were honest, I didn't really have a destination.

"Well, tomorrow I'm going to detox. I just can't take anymore."

Carlos just laughed. "Detox? Get the fuck out of here. You'll never change!"

His words stung, but I couldn't really argue. However, I felt something different this time, like maybe there was a chance for Freddie Jay. I didn't get off to a good start. Within the hour, I had spent the forty bucks Cindy gave me and was high as a kite. Carlos had promised to take me to detox in the morning, but I couldn't stay at his house because his wife wouldn't allow it. There was always an excuse, but here's the truth, some people get high and then run back home to their lives and their jobs. Me, when I get high, it is my life. I'm balls to the wall. There's no half measures and no brakes. I head toward destruction at the speed of death!

I called Carlos in the morning from a stranger's cell phone. No answer. I was standing in front of a gas station on Market Street in downtown Wilmington at 6:00 a.m., having spent the night in the park hiding from a group of kids who were out "bum stomping." It was eight to ten teenagers who would find a homeless guy and beat the hell out of him for kicks. I stayed away from the usual homeless spots to avoid these kids because I know the end of that story. You either get beat up by ten of them or you grab one and beat the hell out of him while his buddies run off. Then the cops lock you up while his mother is screaming about what a good boy he is. If he's black, you get charged with a hate crime! Anyway, it's best to avoid it if you can because it's a lose-lose situation.

Carlos wasn't answering and I had no money left, but this is the way it is with junkies. The day before, Carlos promised to take me to detox, if I would just buy him a bag tonight. Sounds like the Popeye and Wimpy deal: "I will gladly pay you on Tuesday for a hamburger today!" Well, it was payday, and Carlos was stiffing me.

I walked over to an old friend's house. She opened the door just a crack. "Can you give me bus money to get to detox?" She closed the door without a word, and I sat down on her step and lit a cigarette trying to plan my next move. I heard the door open and there stood my friend with money in her hand. "Please get some help," she said as she kissed me, put the money in my hand and closed the door. Tears sprang to my eyes as I headed for the bus. Just then I saw my friend James and his wife riding past. I ran over to the car. "Hey, can you give me a ride to Kirkwood?" I asked quickly.

"Sure, man, jump in."

I jumped in the car and was grateful because this couple never helped anyone but themselves. "Do you wanna do a bag or two before you go?" James asked holding up a bundle of dope. Here's a guy who wouldn't give a dying man a drink of water offering me a ride and dope. I can only attribute my next words to God because I couldn't believe I said it myself.

"Well, doing dope would kinda defeat going to detox wouldn't it?"

"Shit, I've been there seven times. They might not medicate you for twenty-four hours." His words hit like a sledgehammer. I didn't think much of being in total withdrawal for twenty-four hours! For whatever reason, I stuck to my guns and passed on the dope, even with James telling me how good it was.

I reported to detox and voiced my concerns to the nurse who was checking me in. "It's true. We sometimes wait twenty-four hours to medicate certain people, but that's because they come in high and think we can't tell. We are not in the business of overdosing people," she said in a conversational tone. "It's very obvious that you are in full withdrawal, and I'm sure you'll be medicated directly." She was right. Within two hours I was done the paperwork, dressed in hospital scrubs and called into see the doctor. After seeing the doctor, I went to the nurses station where I patiently waited for the nurse to hand me a small cup with an orange pill inside.

"Slip this under your tongue and let it fully dissolve." I did as instructed and the taste was terrible, but the effect was immediate. The drug called Suboxone kept the willies away. I couldn't believe it. I felt no withdrawal at all as they lowered my dose each day over the course of six days.

Allow me to back up just a bit, because I'm getting ahead of myself. It's important to point out that while at detox my second addiction would come to light. Detox in Delaware is coed and it has to be since they only have one facility in the whole state. They wonder why the courts are loaded with theft and prostitution, but in their infinite wisdom, they closed down one of the two detox centers in the entire state. So on my second day at detox in walked my poison in the form of a long-legged blonde with a figure hospital scrubs just couldn't hide. I knew she noticed me, but I employed one of my oldest ploys—I acted as if she didn't exist. All the guys were going crazy over the new blonde, but I paid her absolutely no attention. If there's one thing a pretty girl can't stand it's someone who doesn't notice how pretty she is.

By her second day, she couldn't stand it anymore, so she walked up to me. "Everyone has introduced themselves to me, except you."

I looked at her and smiled my most disarming smile. She returned my smile, but it quickly faded when I said, "Excuse me, I have to speak to the nurse" and walked past her.

The third day she was out of cigarettes and used it as an excuse to approach me. "Hey, Hollywood, do you think I could have one of your cigarettes?" she asked, pleased with the clever little name she gave me. I just nodded to the nurse to give her one of my cigarettes and headed to the smoke area. She was hot on my heels. "Don't you wanna know why I call you Hollywood?" she said smiling, and my God was she cute. By the end of the night, I found a blind spot behind the door in the smoke area and had one of the guys looking for the nurse while the blonde serviced me. I didn't realize it then, but I wasn't only a heroin addict—I was a sex addict, too.

## Chapter 41
## Lord of the Thighs

I would carry on with the blonde till the day of my discharge. I didn't have much of a plan when I left detox, but one of the counselors suggested a rehab in Wilmington. I won't give the name, but it is a free rehab that asks residents to work forty hours a week in the warehouse sorting clothes and goods that they sell in a thrift store to carry the cost of keeping you. I didn't think much of working all week for five bucks, but I didn't have anywhere to go, so I agreed.

The first thirty days of the program you are on what's called blackout—no phone calls, no visits and you're not allowed outside the building. After that, you progress in phases till you graduate. The program is six months and allows you to integrate yourself into the recovery community. It wants you to make meetings on the outside to establish the contact you'll need when you return to the community. As you go through the phases, you are given more and more freedom, including day passes and weekends home. The building itself has men on one side and women on the other. There are fewer women, so their side is much smaller than the men's side. Downstairs are classrooms, a dining room, and a TV area. You can go outside to smoke at certain times. There's also a gazebo and volleyball court. Upstairs there's a computer room, another TV room, a central bathroom with showers and laundry facilities. There are sleeping quarters upstairs, as well; you start out in a six-man room, but as you progress you're moved to a four-man room and finally a two-man room that has its own private showers.

The program itself is intensive with breakfast starting at six, then its morning devotions and work therapy. The evening is classes and meetings according to your phase. You're not allowed to speak to the girls at all. Many people are asked to leave because of relationships. You are free to leave the program at any time, and if you don't follow the rules, you will be tossed out. It's a heavily religious program and while you don't have to be a believer, church and devotions are required of everyone. They feed you well and charge you nothing. Your work therapy pays for your stay. You're assigned a counselor and a work detail your very first day. You can be kicked out for any reason the counselor or captains see fit without any form of defense or appeal. They frown heavily on fraternization and that will get you kicked out fast!

To say I got off to a bad start is a huge understatement! My counselor couldn't stand me and let it show, but I'm to blame for his early opinion of me. I came to the program from the streets and while I was out there I was sleeping in my shoes. As a result my, shoes stunk and the guys in my six-man room were not happy. I was assigned the job of sorting clothes and putting them on hangers to go to the thrift store. On my second day, a guy found a pair of new white on white Air Jordan's, so I took my old stinky shoes off and put the new shoes on. What I didn't know was that the guys who work security look for that sorta thing. It's worth noting that security is guys in the program that have either proven themselves trustworthy or sucked up to the powers that be. So as I was coming back from work, my counselor, Jim, and the resident supervisor pulled me into one of the classrooms. "Where did you get the shoes?" Jim began. I started to lie, but he said words that hit me hard. "How can you steal from the very people who are trying to help you?" I just hung my head in shame, and I think it was my contrition that kept me from being kicked out. "I can see you feel bad and there will be consequences, but you won't be thrown out." Jim said with a little smile. I was very grateful and silently vowed not to disappoint Jim anymore.

Wait, what just happened? I was concerned about disappointing this guy I hardly knew when my whole life was one huge disappointment? Strange things were taking place; strange things indeed! The next day I had my first official meeting with Jim and came clean about everything. I admitted I had a warrant for violation of probation. It was old, but I wanted to face everything. We got on the phone right away and my probation officer said I could stay in the program till she heard from the judge. This was unusual to say the least, but I was really shocked when the judge agreed to let me stay and instructed me to turn myself in upon completion of the program. I apologized to Jim and asked him if we could start over. He was reluctant at first, but came to be one of the most important people on my support team and remains a dear friend to this day.

I bought into the program completely and started giving my full effort to the altruistic program. I helped my peers with book work and listened to their hopes and fears. I worked the steps and took an active role in my recovery. I was given a better job and moved to a four-man room in my first month. I made up my mind not to mess with the girls in the program. I waited to get to phase two and became notorious in the rooms of Narcotics Anonymous. I got quite a reputation as a playboy and enjoyed the title. I had guys in phase one asking if they could go to meetings with me as soon as they were allowed just to get my cast-offs. Only Jim had the courage to ask me about the addiction that I wasn't addressing, my addiction to sex. I had to admit that I was addicted to sex and started taking that fearless moral inventory. It was scary to really look at myself, but it's also necessary. I was replacing heroin with sex. It was just another way to feel good. I set about addressing all my addictions, and it's an ongoing process.

I started living again. I began to believe in myself. On a day pass, I went to the beach and had a blast. I was learning to live without drugs, and it was glorious. I became a trusted member at the program and things were going great. My sponsor took me to Maryland to visit my mother, who was now in an assisted-living home suffering from the early stages of Alzheimer's. I'll never forget the smile on her face when I walked in that day. I took her a big stuffed animal and some of her favorite snacks. I had on a collared shirt and tie. She cried and questioned whether I was "really" clean, but in her heart she knew I was. My mother lived for two more years, and she left this world knowing that her youngest son was drug free and OK. As my sponsor and I were leaving, I said to him, "I wish I could do something to make up for all the wrong I've done to that old lady."

He looked me in the eye and said, "You just did."

## Chapter 42
## Changes

I felt great. I had never amassed any clean time. There were times in prison when I wasn't using, but this was my first time having true sobriety. I loved everything about recovery: the feeling of self-worth and the camaraderie of others in the same struggle. I learned that helping others was a major key to staying clean, and I grabbed hold of it early on. My counselor Jim was riding to work one day and saw me walking down the street reading from the A.A. Big Book. People around me were complaining about the rehab, and the biggest gripe was "Work therapy," but I was grateful to have a nice bed to climb into. I didn't mind the work if they were giving me life! I never understood the people that complained, and I still don't. No one is holding you; you can walk out the door at any time. You're in no way a prisoner. If you're reading this book in a rehab, I'd implore you to find the things to be grateful for and stop bitching about the unfair things or what you see as favoritism. Keep the focus on you because within a year, you won't know 95% of the people around you right now!

They gave me a job in the kitchen, and I was incredibly happy to get away from the clothes and the females in the program who worked with you, but you weren't supposed to talk to them. Look, I won't slam the program I credit with saving my life, but there's some big flaws in it. Here's the deal—they do so much good that these flaws can be overlooked. There are those who want to blame the program for this or that, but it's designed to modify your behavior. That's all I'm going to say. If you know a better way to get clean, write a book about it or whatever. As for me, I'm eternally grateful to the army of angels that took me in when no one else would. It was there I found salvation and a new way of life. If you can't figure out what that program is, go back and read between the lines.

My first sponsor was my counselor Jim's roommate. I chose him to sponsor me because I wanted Jim to like me, but I came to love my sponsor like a little brother. I know that sounds weird, but I can't help the way things worked out. Travis had about four years clean when I met him. He was one of the first people I met at the program. He brought a Sunday night voluntary meeting together, and I would attend because Travis had an easygoing manner and seemed interested in me. At first I thought maybe he was homosexual, but that wasn't the case. He loved the program and stayed connected by helping the newcomer. Travis started sponsoring me, but I leaped past him in short order. He had more clean time, but I was a literature fanatic and was being asked to sponsor people before I left rehab. I didn't sponsor anyone for a year, but Travis and I were inseparable. He even got me a job at his shop as soon as I finished rehab.

Now let me back up just a bit. I had my probation officer come to the program, and she loved it, Jim made a great impression. He's incredibly professional and easy to like. I was kinda bummed out that upon my completion of the program I was to be arrested for violation of probation even though she liked what I was doing. Once the judge issues a warrant, that's it— you must go in front of him to answer for your violation. I graduated the program in seven months. My girlfriend, my sister, my sponsor and Jim (who came in on his day off) watched me graduate. It was amazing to me, considering it was just seven months before that I was picking cigarettes from the gutter. As I looked out at the faces before me, I was choked with emotion. I was so grateful to be at that podium and not in active addiction that the tears streamed down my face. The speech I prepared went out the window. I just thanked everyone and said a few words before accepting my certificate of completion and tie pin from the directors of the program. It's worth noting that the directors of the rehab were a husband and wife who I left out of this book because I think they would want that, but this book would not be written if it weren't for those two people. I'll simply say this to Mr. and Mrs. Diaz—no child could love his parents as much as I love you. Thank you so much for all that you have done and continue to do.

There were still many battles to face, but for that day I was king. Never had I been loved and respected for doing the right thing. I was on a cloud, and I can't say it never burst. Yes, troubles and pain would come, but I was never in a better position to deal with those things. I've learned how to be happy in spite of troubles, and that is priceless. I will share that with you soon; keep reading. After I graduated I had to turn myself in, so I packed my things and headed down to the probation office on Monday morning. As we waited for the police to take me into custody, I sat and talked to my probation officer who couldn't get over the fact that I had a suit on to come see her. The police officer walked in and said, "Where's your client?" He thought I was a lawyer bringing my client to turn himself in. We all laughed as I explained I was my client. They didn't handcuff me and the officer who transported me let me sit up front, I actually just walked over and got in as if we were old friends. The officer asked a lot of questions, and it turned out his son was addicted to drugs. When that officer led me to the jail cell, we stopped to pray together for his son, I'm proud to say I gave him some phone numbers and would later meet his son. His son is doing great these days. God is awesome!

The next day was a holiday, so I had to lie in jail for a few days. The last time that judge saw me I had hair down to the middle of my back, weighed around 165 and was a complete mess. When I went before him in a suit and tie, with close-cropped hair and weighing 195, he was amazed. More than that, he saw something different in me and closed my case out. That doesn't happen often. When you violate probation, you usually go to jail for whatever term your probation or suspended sentence was in the first place. I walked out of the courtroom with my case closed out and free and clear of more probation. Very unusual indeed, but didn't I tell you my God is awesome!!

## Chapter 43
## My Sacrifice

After some wrangling, Jim got me into the crossover house. This house is reserved for those who do really well in the rehab and have found employment. For a guy who couldn't find a job before, I now had a few options and took the one my sponsor offered. I wish I had taken the other, but I went with the higher-paying job. The next six months would bring so many changes. I was still struggling with sex addiction in a big way, but here's the funny thing about sex addiction—it's difficult to diagnose a healthy libido from sexual compulsion. I had three or four girls I was having regular sex with and when I wasn't, I was watching porn or reading pornographic material. It was an addiction. It had to be addressed, and I went about it the same way I did my heroin addiction. I put all my pornography in a duffel bag and stopped seeing the girls I was dating. I went totally without sex for thirty days, which for me was a small miracle by itself.

Like the alcoholic who keeps a bottle in the cabinet, I couldn't bring myself to throw my porn away, but I did stop viewing it. I suffered in silence because there was no one to talk to without them making a joke of it, and even writing this chapter I'm a bit embarrassed. However, if it helps another it's worth it. I prayed and fasted and read what I could about it, then the famous Freddie Jay temper would surface and nearly derail all I had worked for. The fellow who was the house manager got to his position by kissing ass. I'll call him Keith. I did my best to get along with him, but he was the resident supervisor when I was in the program. He was getting people put out for relationships, yet his girlfriend graduated with high praise. I don't like a hypocrite. Anyway, he came in one night and woke me up to yell at me for leaving a towel in the bathroom. He's lucky he did it from a distance because when I came out of the room I was ready to kick his fat ass. He started up the steps, but stopped when he saw I was at the top of the stairs already. He quickly ran to his room and called my counselor Jim. Everyone knew that Jim was one of a few people on the planet that could yell at me and get away with it.

The issue passed, but I knew I had to get on the ball and stack some chips to get an apartment. Even with the little problems that would pop up now and then, my life was much better than it ever had been. I felt in control of my life, like I had direction. Hope was now a constant companion. It had eluded me for so long, but now anything was possible. My addictions were in check, and I was working on something. Making meetings, doing step work and attending church twice a week was impacting my life in a big way. I was evolving at an incredible rate. I would walk down to the train station every morning and take the R2 to work, and in the evening, Travis would drop me off at the crossover house. Travis and I were always hanging out, making meetings and doing this or that, though I found Travis to be a very different person at work. And while I had a great deal of respect for him, I didn't like working for him.

Travis was still holding the Sunday night meeting at the

center, and I went with him most Sundays. It was at that meeting that my life would head in a brand new direction, one I never saw coming! I had my compulsions in check. I was working the steps and living a life I only dreamed of. I was a tax-paying citizen with a decent job and the love and respect of my peers. I had friends I could count on and my family ties were slowly being rebuilt. My sister was 100% in my corner and my niece wrote a paper for school of which I was the focal point. It was titled "My Hero". Even my sister's adult son, who was slow to forgive, had contacted Travis to ask him if I was really clean. He and I are very close again, and he's one of my favorite people on the planet. As for the sexual addiction, I found a support group and a therapist, and I've learned how to live a porn-free life, to have love for myself and to view women as beautiful creatures of God and not as sex objects. I have female friends today who I love and respect, and they are my extended family now.

I alluded to a new direction in life at Travis's Sunday night meeting. I had always prided myself on not dating a girl in the rehab. I never wanted to be responsible for someone leaving or returning to a drug lifestyle. I watched many relationships start there, only to see them living on the streets within a few weeks or so. I really was just working on myself and not looking for love when April walked into the meeting that night. She had long blond hair, big blue eyes and a figure that would knock you off your feet. Travis would later say that I looked like I was hit by lightening, and I gotta say I felt like it! I asked her name, and she said April. I tried to look casual, but my heart skipped a beat when she smiled. At church that Sunday, she wore a dress and every guy in there was thinking less than godly thoughts. There were other guys interested in her, but I put a stop to it in short order. Everyone knew I was crazy about the little blonde, including her. When she came off restriction, I took her to an outside meeting and on the side of the church, I kissed her for the first time. I was hooked.

It was a great time in my life, one of the best! I was saving money, I had a promotion on the way at work and I was in love. Every morning it was a joy to wake up. I awoke one Friday morning and went to work, and even Travis couldn't get under my skin because this was the weekend April would get her day pass and we were going to spend the day together. I collected my paycheck and headed home, I was planning the best day I could put together for April when my phone went off. In an instant all my plans came crashing down. It was April. She had left the program and was going home to her mother's house in New Jersey. I asked her to wait till I got there before she took the train home and she agreed. This was the worst possible news. Not only was the girl I fell in love with leaving the program, she was going to another state.

## Chapter 44
## Curtain Call

I got Travis to drop me off at the bus station. There she stood with three hefty bags full of clothes and she was furious. "Why did you leave?" I asked, all business.

She teared up and my business attitude went out the window. "It's the warehouse guy. He came on to me and when I told him I was there to work on myself and wasn't interested in a relationship, he started writing me up. He wrote me up twice this week, and I can't take it!" She fell against my chest sobbing. I knew the guy she was talking about. He name was Alfredo and he loved bullying people on the line. I had threatened him once and he backed off, knowing that I'd catch him at an outside meeting and he left me alone, but he didn't know April was with me. If she had come to me I could have stopped all of that, but now it was too late.

"How much is your bus?" I asked, always the hero.

"I have the money; the problem is there are no more busses today."

So my brain is in overdrive. I don't want to offend her, but it looks like a hotel room is the only answer till morning. She was very hesitant, and I liked that. She said she would just stay at the bus station. I explained the kind of people that wander around that area after dark, so she reluctantly agreed, and I checked her into a hotel near my sister's house. The plan was to get something to eat and then I'd go to Cindy's and come back in the morning to get her on the bus to New Jersey. I never made it to my sister's house, and we didn't sleep a wink. In the morning, I put her on a train instead of the bus and we made promises to each other.

The relationship started with either her coming to Delaware for the weekend or us staying in New York for the weekend. We had plans to get an apartment, but her mother was taking a chunk of her paycheck to live there while her mother's husband—all whacked out on Xanax and vodka—shouted obscenities at April for using the phone or anything else his drug-addled brain deemed worthy of a barrage of insults. I was stacking chips, but I had rent at crossover house and by now I had bought cell phones for April and me. I hated when she called me and her drunken mother and stepfather were fighting in the background. I knew I had to get April out of that environment, but things were progressing slowly.

Things were kicked into high gear by two events: one came when April's mother asked April to get her a bag of dope. What kind of woman ask her daughter, who's in recovery, to get her some drugs? This baffled me nearly as much as how she allowed her husband to call April such disgusting names. I doubt if April's mother will read this book, but I make no apologies for what's written here because it's the gospel truth. It's my opinion that she didn't want April to succeed. She likes looking down on people because it makes her feel better about herself. If I had to say something nice about the woman, that's a tough one, but she did divorce that loser guy and married a guy who seems to be a good man, but that's the best I can do.

The second thing came about two days after April told

me about her mother asking her to get drugs for her. April was working two jobs and I was taking all the overtime I could get, so it was a rare Friday when I got off at four o'clock. I was sitting on the porch with my friends Ricky and Denny when my cell phone went off. It was April and she was very upset. I calmed her down and asked her what had happened. "I don't want you to think I did this on purpose!" she said. My brain started to race. What happened? Had she used drugs? Had she cheated on me? I was trying to make sense of her words when two little words came through and hit me like high- velocity bullet. "I'm pregnant!"

I went silent as she started rambling. She was concerned I would think she was trying to trap me. I was stunned silent. I could hear her 'other's slurred voice in the background. "You ain't bringing a fuckin' kid in this house!"

I quickly gathered my composure when April asked me what I wanted to do. "What do you mean? There's only one option! We had planned on getting an apartment, and now we just have to work harder to get it done sooner. Abortion isn't on the table at all for me, but how do you feel about it?" I asked in my matter-of-fact tone.

"Freddie, I want the baby, but I don't want you to feel like you have to be with me because I got pregnant."

This revelation made me swallow some pride. I borrowed money from Ricky and from my sister and within a month, with help from Travis, I got my apartment! Then they all lived happily ever after!!?? I wish that were the case, but it isn't. There have been problems along the way; slip-ups, failures and loss arise from time to time. My mom died in December, 2009, from bone cancer. She left this world knowing that her youngest boy was sober, married and had a baby on the way. I'm so glad my mother at least got to see me clean and sober before departing this life. I alluded to slip-ups and I'll touch on that briefly to help the addict in recovery. I went to the hospital with severe headaches and told them I couldn't take narcotics. I tried a number of non-narcotic pills and my headaches wouldn't stop. Finally, between the headaches and an injury to my back, I allowed the doctor to prescribe me Percocet, thinking if I took them as prescribed, I could handle it. I was wrong!

My brain can't tell the difference between an opiate for pain and an opiate for recreation. I got honest very quickly and reached out for help. My honesty caused some in the program to betray me, but I've forgiven them. I quickly got with my doctor and my counselor and my friends in N.A. and A.A. and got it worked out. An ex-junkie who must take pain medicine is a fine line to walk. The irony is that I messed up my body so bad by taking drugs I didn't need, I now need drugs to live a pain-free life. Well, maybe not pain-free, but bearable pain. Anyway, the doctors recommended Methadone. It turns out it's not only used for junkies to stay clean; they are prescribing it more and more for pain management. I won't get into the things I think about "replacement therapy." I'll save that for another book. However, I will say that Methadone has worked for me. There are purists who say being on Methadone really isn't being clean. I say walk a mile in another's shoes before you judge that person. My life is happy and productive, but most importantly, it's manageable. I have a life today that I only dreamed of during my addiction.

## Chapter 45
## This Is the End

Today my life is manageable, and I'm so grateful for all that I have been blessed with. My son was born in March of 2009 and my world again went in a new direction. I fell in love with my little guy the moment I laid eyes on him. My wife became even more beautiful to me when she put that bundle of joy in my arms. I really can't explain it to you, but on the day he was born, the three of us bonded in a way that can only come from a higher power. When we brought him home from the hospital, I would take on the role of Mr. Mom; changing diapers and making bottles became second nature, I'd rush home from work to see what new wonderful thing he had done that day and he has never let me down. There was always a new miracle. I decided to start my own business so I could make my own hours. I did just that, and I have small roofing and siding business that pays the bills, but more importantly gives me lots of time to be a dad.

My oldest son is a very big part of my life. He lives in another state, but we text each other a lot. It took a lot of work, but God has restored our relationship. After a few months of phone calls, as I was about to get off the phone, I told my son I loved him, and one of the most beautiful things you'll ever hear as a parent came through the phone. "I love you, too, Dad." I put the phone down and tears streamed down my face as I sat thanking my higher power. My life is beautiful and I'm truly grateful for every day I'm given, every relationship that has been restored and every prayer ever said for me. There's still plenty of work to be done. I have a middle son who has been fed lots of lies and forced to live a lie calling his grandmother "mom." I leave that to God, I know the time will come when all things work to the greater goal, the bigger picture and ultimately, God's will.

To tie up some loose ends you may be wondering about, my nephew, who threw me out when I stole from him, stood as best man at my wedding. My sister and I are closer than ever. She gave her heart to Jesus in 2009 and is doing great. My oldest brother, the one who killed my father, has finished his sentence in Maryland, but was sent back to South Carolina where he remains incarcerated. My other brother got out of prison, and I tried to reach out to him. We talked for awhile, but old resentments popped up and we had to admit we just don't see eye to eye. He lives with a girlfriend somewhere in Maryland. We don't talk much, but we never really were close. I know the book is supposed to have a happy ending, but the truth is it has a human ending. There's still much work to be done and life has its ups and downs. I'm happy mostly because I choose to be happy, and I choose to be happy because I've been given the greatest gift in the world. That gift is one more day clean.

I continue to work the steps and meet with a counselor a few times a month. My work with other addicts will continue because I believe that I can only keep what I have by giving it away. My hope for this book is that it reaches those who feel hopeless and gives them the strength to get through it, to let God enter into your life and take all those things meant for bad and turn them into something great! I'll close with a quote by Oswald Chambers: "If through a broken heart God can bring His purpose to pass, then thank Him for breaking your heart."

www.ingramcontent.com/pod-product-compliance
Lightning Source LLC
Chambersburg PA
CBHW071456040426
42444CB00008B/1361